MY SOUL LOOKS BACK

A Memoir

JESSICA B. HARRIS

SCRIBNER

New York   London   Toronto   Sydney   New Delhi

Scribner
An Imprint of Simon & Schuster, Inc.
1230 Avenue of the Americas
New York, NY 10020

First Scribner hardcover edition May 2017

SCRIBNER and design are registered trademarks of The Gale Group, Inc., used
under license by Simon & Schuster, Inc., the publisher of this work.

For information about special discounts for bulk purchases, please contact Simon
& Schuster Special Sales at 1-866-506-1949 or business@simonandschuster.com.

The Simon & Schuster Speakers Bureau can bring authors to your live event. For
more information or to book an event, contact the Simon & Schuster Speakers
Bureau at 1-866-248-3049 or visit our website at www.simonspeakers.com.

Interior design by Jill Putorti

Manufactured in the United States of America

10 9 8 7 6 5 4 3 2 1

ISBN 978-1-5011-2590-4
ISBN 978-1-5011-2700-7 (ebook)

For those who knew me then
And those who knew me when
And those who know me now

You cannot step twice in the same river.

HERACLITUS

CONTENTS

RECIPES

MY SOUL
LOOKS BACK

PROLOGUE

My man is
Black Golden Amber
Changing.
Warm mouths of Brandy Fine . . .

So opens Maya Angelou's poem "To a Man." If I'd read those lines back in the 1970s, this story would never have happened. Instead, ignorant, trusting, believing in love, and woefully too young, I raced in. I've been rereading Angelou's poetry recently because her passing has brought memories of my youth vividly back, like Léon Damas's long-held-in hiccup. I relive them again and again.

I've been known to say that I am the Zelig of the second half of the twentieth century because it has been my great good fortune to turn up in multiple special spots. I lived and studied in Paris when Les Halles was still going strong and the buildings were gray, I've supped with Sembène in Senghor's Senegal, and I've danced in the Candomblé ring in Jorge Amado's Bahia. However, the real reason that I identify with the Woody Allen character is that it was my privilege to spend part of my youth with Maya Angelou, James Baldwin, and their circles of friends as they were becoming icons of twentieth-century America. Their joy in one another, the fierceness of their intellectual pursuits, and their absolute dedication to civil rights and to the righting of civil wrongs of all sorts made their names hallmarks of honesty and totems for truth that influenced the world.

I am not central to the story, although I have lived it; rather, it is about an extraordinary circle of friends who came together, lived outrageously, loved abundantly, laughed uproariously, and savored life while they created work that would come to define the era. That they knew one another was interesting; that they partied together, savored one another's company, encouraged one another's endeavors, celebrated one another's achievements, and mourned one another's losses is extraordinary.

This tale is also the story of a city. New York City, its neighborhoods and its vibrant life, is also a character, for no other place in the world could have spawned and celebrated their lives with such intensity. Paris had the belle epoque, the 1920s, and the existentialist 1950s; London had the swinging sixties, and New York City in the early 1970s was the hub-of-the-universe city. It was a city in the throes of a major transition, when restaurants could offer a glimpse into the fading world of café society or bubble with the excitement of the new era that was being created, and the clubs that existed for every possible social stripe throbbed nightly with the excesses of the sexual and moral revolution that had been ushered in in the 1960s. Life was lived in wide-screen Technicolor in ways that had never before existed. It was the city before AIDS and economic downturns made it a very different place. Memory has muted some of the vibrancy of the colors, and the dates fade into a continuum, but the vitality of the friendships, the commitment to activism, and the joie de vivre of those heady days remain as palpable as the intertwined connective tissue of the lives that were lived then.

James Baldwin was at the center of this circle of friends. His huge presence radiated warmth and intensity; his cultural and political stature at that point in time was enormous. Through my young eyes, being in Baldwin's circle, however tangentially, felt at times as though all were in attendance at the court of a very reluctant sun king. Although the group was egalitarian, there was an unspoken hierarchy, and everyone sort of knew exactly where they fit in.

If Baldwin was the pivot of the literary court, his trusted second was a gentleman and a gentle man from Durham, North Carolina, named Samuel Clemens Floyd III: Angelou's Amber Sam. Floyd's name's literary allusion to Mark Twain was prescient, for Sam had been one of the early

Black writers on staff at *Newsweek* and was the director of faculty and curriculum and taught English in the higher-education opportunity program, SEEK, at Queens College, where I also worked. Like Candomblé's Orixa Ogun, breaker of bonds who clears paths and builds roads, it was Sam who opened the way into the circle of friends for me and led me down the rabbit hole into the wonderland that was that moment in time.

Chapter One

CLUB 81—SAMMY AND JIMMY

It's boarded and shuttered now, with windows taped as though for an impending hurricane or a wrecking ball: a relic of another time. Those who know the Meatpacking District from *Sex and the City* hurry by on their way to the High Line and the trendy restaurants or window-shop at the Louboutin shop across the street, but occasionally a passerby stops and stares into the blank windows as though recalling another time: a time before the area had a name, when this was the farthest outpost of Greenwich Village and there were some West Side blocks where only the brave dared walk because the rats were the size of small dogs. The Village then was a grittier place, but one that was equally vibrant with its own life. Beyond the building at the corner of Horatio and Greenwich Streets, farther up the street, West Street and the Hudson River loomed with meatpacking warehouses, single-room-occupancy hotels, hookers, johns, pickup bars, and nighttime cruising haunts for the gay population that had come out of the collective closet only a decade or so earlier.

Then, this now-abandoned building was a beacon, a way station. Filtered light puddled on the corner outside its windows, the hum of conversation poured out the door, and on weekends the sounds of guitar music and singing could be heard as the *tuna* (singing groups from various Spanish universities) made their ways through the bar throngs singing Spanish college songs for tips. Then, if one lost the way, all that was required was a sense of smell. It didn't have to be particularly good, for even those without acute olfactory nerves could recognize the aroma of garlic wafting from the kitchen. If you followed the pungent fragrance down the street, El Faro beckoned. It was a West Village landmark signaling safe passage to travelers like the lighthouse for which it was named.

Reputed to be the first Spanish restaurant in New York City, El Faro sat on the corner at the nether end of the "respectable" Village. Vivian Kramer described it in 1969 in the *Greenwich Village Cookbook*:

El Faro is a small Spanish restaurant tucked away in the western part of Greenwich Village, well off the beaten track. The prices are moderate and the menu includes paellas and other rice dishes, as well as spareribs from northwestern Spain, which is where the owner comes from. One followed another, and fellow Galicians are still migrating to join the kitchen and dining room staff.

The dining room is mostly tables and chairs—the emphasis here is definitely on food. The walls are decorated with life-sized portraits, like storybook illustrations, that do have a certain Spanish look, but, because of the food, nobody seems to pay much attention to the atmosphere.

The phone rings frequently. Many of the callers are would-be customers who have lost their way. The owners give directions, but no reservations—the management just can't promise to serve everyone who wants to eat there on a given night.

Kramer captures some of the atmosphere, but she doesn't convey the sense of surprise that many had when happening upon the dappled light streaming from El Faro's doorway at what then seemed to be the end of the known world. Nor does she give a sense of the stygian decor of dark wood and stained glass that prevailed in the front room near the bar. El Faro was a hub; astonishingly cacophonous, it bustled nightly with the activity of neighborhood folks for whom it represented one of the few dining options. They packed the place along with others who came from afar to sample delicacies such as barbecued pork with almond sauce and shrimp with green sauce and partridge Spanish-style and *pollo al ajillo* (chicken with garlic) washed down with pitchers brimming with a heady sangria.

Those in the know or with little to spend who wanted something comforting and warming would order the Galician specialty: *caldo gallego*, a hearty kale and sausage soup rich with shredded collard greens and chunks of potato. It was the owner's salute to Galicia, his native corner of Spain, and a bowl made a filling meal. Neighborhood folks who were loved by the management could call for take-out orders by special dispensation, and the back room had booths where folks could hunker down for serious conversations well lubricated with drinks from the full bar.

Kramer does not mention, and perhaps did not know, that the city's famous showed up there on more than one occasion—actors Rip and Geri (Torn and Page); Richie Havens, who lived up the street; writer Dick Schaap (whose daughter Rosie remembers it well); and perhaps the most famous resident of Horatio Street: James Baldwin. I didn't know El Faro and I'd never been to Horatio Street, although I lived in the West Village on Charles Street only a few blocks away. That would all change one afternoon in the early 1970s.

It was a day like any other: I'd finished teaching my French classes at Queens College for the week and was heading down the street to the bus stop to return to my Manhattan apartment when I noticed a colleague in front of me. Awe inspiring in his intellect, with a notably acid tongue, he was the terror of the college's SEEK Program, where his rants about pedagogy were legendary and kept the program on the academic high road. He was also the bad boy of the English department, where he taught some of the first courses the college ever offered in African American literature; the professors there admired his erudition. I was therefore astonished walking along behind him one afternoon to watch him surreptitiously as he capered down the street like a playful kid (in both literal and colloquial senses of the word). We met up at the corner and, chatting collegially, found out that we lived within blocks of each other in the West Village. I was nonetheless astounded when he asked me to stop by his place for a drink.

We walked companionably and talked about everything from Village life to SEEK matters, the French courses I was teaching to things more personal. Sam began what would become a running joke, teasing me about my mother, who also worked at Queens College, albeit in another department and as a lowly administrative assistant, hounding him to make sure that the job I had been promised remained mine on my return from a year in France. To hear him tell it, she was a terror, and I giggled recognizing her single-mindedness in all things that concerned me, her only child.

We both lived in a Greenwich Village that was in transition from the bohemian outpost where the grandmothers of those who'd made it in Little Italy lived alongside the artists and writers of another era. I lived on Charles Street right off Greenwich Avenue, the first tenant in an old-line tenement that had just been renovated into luxury apartments as part of the Village's ongoing gentrification. We got off at West Fourth Street, my stop, as I had some things to drop off at my apartment before heading over to his.

Near the subway exit at Eighth Street at the corner of Sixth Avenue (no New Yorker has ever called it Avenue of the Americas), the Women's House of Detention still loomed gloomily, although it had been closed in 1971. Longtime Villagers recalled the street theater created by the women prisoners yelling from the windows down to their friends, pimps, and passersby on the streets and the replies shouted up. I remembered the prison from Angela Davis's brief incarceration there and trials of the Black Panther activists that marked its last years. The tall red-brick edifice dominated the corner and had housed a range of prisoners from Polly Adler to Ethel Rosenberg to Grace Paley, and included Afeni Shakur who was two months' pregnant with Tupac at the time of her sequester. It was torn down in 1973 and replaced by a garden, creating a deceptively peaceful memorial to the women who'd suffered there. Across the street on Sixth Avenue, Balducci's, an old-line Italian greengrocer, offered vegetables and fruit at a time before every other Manhattan corner boasted a Korean market. Old man Balducci had taken a liking to me and always slipped an orange or two or a grapefruit into my bag when I shopped there.

Small eateries catered to the neighborhood denizens and to those who headed to the Village for their weekend dose of bohemia. Many were red-sauce Italian like Angelina's on Greenwich Avenue around the corner from my apartment, where Angelina, someone's Italian *nonna*, terrified the kitchen and presided over the dining room greeting those she knew warmly and banishing others to the outer reaches. Other spots like Jai Alai, La Bilbaína, Café Valencia, and Sevilla were Spanish in the model of El Faro, each boasting variants of the shrimp in green sauce and spare ribs in almond sauce served in the same clay *cazuelas* and brimming aluminum cauldrons that the Horatio Street restaurant had made famous. And still others were steak houses and fine-dining establishments like Casey's, the Coach House, and Charles French Restaurant. There was even a good representation of international restaurants serving cuisines from Middle Eastern to Japanese to Jamaican.

Greenwich Village in the early 1970s was divided into

several neighborhoods. The West Village, the main residential area, ran from Sixth to Eighth Avenues and from Fourteenth Street down to Houston Street. (A snootier section ran east of Sixth Avenue over to Fifth Avenue and was simply called Greenwich Village.) Eighth Street was the main shopping drag and boasted record shops with bins of vinyl discs including the Nonesuch ones of what would be later called World Beat Music, Brentano's sold books, and on MacDougal, a side street, Fred Leighton sold frothy Mexican wedding dresses that I loved but couldn't afford, long before he moved uptown to sell the antique jewelry that now adorns red-carpet denizens at Oscar time. Bleecker Street east of Sixth Avenue housed spots like the Village Gate, which hosted Latin musicians and jazz greats, and showcased some of the remaining beatnik coffee houses like Caffé Reggio and Le Figaro Café in the pre-Starbucks era.

There were small off-Broadway theaters like the Circle in the Square; *The Fantasticks* at the Sullivan Street Playhouse had already been running for a decade. West of Seventh near West Tenth at 340 Bleecker there was Boomers, a jazz club that had amazing musical brunches and lethal Bloody Marys. It was so much a part of downtown Black life that it was even featured in the film *Superfly*. Nearby, the Pink Teacup provided hearty breakfasts complete with grits for jazz-loving night crawlers of the dawn patrol and soul food—fried chicken, smothered pork chops, and catfish—for nostalgic southerners. On Seventh Avenue, the Village Vanguard and other spots made the area known for jazz hangouts. A few short blocks to the south and the east, NYU offered the Collegiate Village. It was then contained in the zone around Washington Square Park, which still could be a nightly no-man's-land. By day, though, the Village was every young girl's *That Girl* dream and I knew all of those sections.

But Sam and I left the Village I was familiar with, headed down Greenwich Avenue, and rounded the corner to Horatio Street, where the wind howling from the Hudson River seemed to chill things by several degrees and indicate that this was a different part of the Village—a wilder zone. We stopped in front of a Federal-era building at number 81 around the corner from the spot where Alexander Hamilton died following his duel with Aaron Burr. The building had been a private house in those days; in more recent times, it had been carved into multiple apartments. This was where Sam lived in what I would learn had formerly been James Baldwin's building. They had been neighbors; that's how their friendship began.

He opened the door, and I was delighted to see the swish of a cat's tail as Monsieur Blues, a sleek round-headed blue-point Siamese, wandered over to greet Sam and nose around my feet, no doubt smelling my own Siamese cats. Blues, I would later learn, was Sam's familiar, his confidant, and his solace. I settled in on the circa-1950s couch, and Sam took up residence in his throne by the window, he nursing a J&B scotch with a splash of water and me a glass of red wine.

As we sat and chatted, Sam shed his gruff Queens College persona and eased into himself. He lit up one of the Gauloise Bleues he smoked obsessively, creating the fragrance mixture that would forever mean Sam Floyd to me—Chanel Pour Homme and French black tobacco—and talked of African American literature and opera, politics and cooking, and golf. I was intrigued and entranced by the breadth of his knowledge on so many disparate things.

We hit it off, and a few weeks later, I invited him to join me at a dinner party I was giving at the Spring Street loft of a friend who was a dress designer. I've always loved hosting sit-down dinners with multiple courses, a raft of china and glassware, a tablecloth, linen napkins, and place cards. This was one such extravaganza laid out on the working loft's cutting tables. I've long forgotten the menu, but I remember that the dessert was *orange givré*, a recipe that I'd cribbed from the bill of fare at the Paris Drugstore Saint Germain. There, it consisted of a hollowed-out orange filled with orange sorbet and then refrozen. In New York, there was no sorbet then, and the only sherbet available was raspberry, and it was a vivid blood red that made the result more *grand guignol* than *grande cuisine*. It certainly ended the evening with a flourish. To my delight, Sam came, ate and drank well, and behaved well, verbally challenging a few of my friends. At the end of the evening, he even waited to accompany me home. I have a dim memory of Sam starting an argument with my friend who'd graciously agreed to hold the party in her loft, accusing her of being a sellout and not politically aware. That should have been a warning note, but the clanging of those bells was lost in my glow of a successful dinner party, and out I swept on a love-besotted cloud, heading back to my Charles Street apartment with Sam, who'd actually waited for me until after the cleanup was done. That was the beginning. We first slept together that night, finding comfort and companionship in each other in a wine-sodden haze. In time, our nascent friendship turned into deeper affection and then into something stronger, and eventually we were acknowledged to be a couple.

Sam had the ability to transform the ordinary into the special: transmute the dross of daily life into magical moments of spun gold. He'd taken to occasionally stopping off after work in midtown at the old Russian Tea Room, when he felt like it and was feeling flush, for champagne, blini, and caviar. Owner Faith Stewart-Gordon used to advertise it on WQXR every morning as being slightly to the left of Carnegie Hall, and it was the kind of spot where you could see émigrés, socialites, and the occasional star like Nureyev. Sam arrived like Grant taking Richmond, occupied one of the coveted booths, commandeered the center of the red leather banquettes, and spent the rest of the afternoon regaling his guests with tall tales and quiet confidences. These forays often evolved into dinner at a nearby restaurant. Each day offered another possibility for exploration, expansion, and delight.

Sam's apartment at 81 Horatio Street was the downtown hub of activity for the group, and he hosted one and all in his small living room in a permanent floating salon where on any given occasion, you might run into fellow academics Corrine Jennings, Richard Long, and Dolly McPherson; writers Maya Angelou, Louise Meriwether, Rosa Guy, and Paule Marshall; actors Rip Torn and Geraldine Page; and just plain friends like Mary Painter and her French chef husband, Georges Garin, or Baldwin himself, though at this point, he'd been spoken of but I'd yet to meet him. Liquor flowed—the three J's: J&B, Jack Daniels, and Johnnie Walker Black. Wine never ran out, and if Sam wasn't cooking, food could be ordered from El Faro up the street. The apartment so bubbled with activity that some of us just referred to it as Club 81.

Entertainments at Club 81 were usually unplanned and just seemed to happen when someone was in town or there was an event of some sort. We'd gather, drinks would be poured, food prepared or ordered, and it was on to the next stop. If Maya were in town, there would be at least one dinner at Paparazzi on the East Side. The Brasserie was another favored spot that recalled the Brasserie Lipp and others in Paris. The grand staircase that bisected the room was suitable for sweeping entrances and offered a perfect vantage point from which to scope out the crowd. The menu featured such Parisian favorites as steak *frites* and *choucroute*, the Alsatian sauerkraut dish that I'd come to love.

I'm still not sure just how or why Sam settled on me; perhaps my naiveté attracted him. I certainly came from another side of his spectrum. I suspect that some things about my family's oh-so-aspirational, oh-so-bourgeois lifestyle reminded him of a quieter, more sedate life that he'd perhaps hankered for in his youth in Durham. I was young, but I had all the trappings of a worldly sophisticate. I could keep up a good conversation about world politics. I was a bona fide bluestocking. I'd read the classics and could quote Proust in the original with a Parisian accent. I loved nothing more than his Sunday sessions when whoever had assembled at Club 81 sat around and read "When Malindy Sings" by Paul Laurence Dunbar in full dialect or acted out snippets of plays directed and stage-managed by Sam, especially Baldwin's *The Amen Corner*, or read poetry from *God's Trombones* by James Weldon Johnson in full-throated voices.

I can still hear Sam's stentorian tones, complete with the rich preacher's cadence of one who has spent more than one Sunday down front on the mourner's bench in a Black church.

Weep not, weep not,
She is not dead;
She's resting in the bosom of Jesus.

I can still see the Angel of Death and hear the horses' hoofs as he journeyed to Yamacraw to take Sister Caroline home:

Go Down Death, and bring her to me.

It wasn't all poetry and parties. Alongside my teaching, I was building a career as a journalist at a string of the newly forming Black magazines. In short, I had been raised by Edwardian-era parents to be perfect midcentury modern wife material: an accommodating helpmate. I loved to entertain, made good conversation, was pretty much game for anything, and as a colleague of Sam's at Queens College had my own money to spend. Just the kind of girl you could easily take home to Mother. I was also fifteen years younger than Sam and so wet behind the ears that the waterfall sounds drowned out any warning signals there might have been. I was quiet, polite, unquestioning, and very well educated: the perfect clay for Sam to mold.

Sam, of course, had been presented to my parents, who were not sure what to think of this volatile suitor who was fifteen years older than their much-coddled daughter.

They were all too pleased that someone seemed to understand the daughter they had spawned who did not fit into
any of the worlds that they knew, but they were decidedly
cautious about his temperament and his age. Sam did not
attempt to curry favor with them. He knew my mother from
Queens College and regarded her as a professional ally in
his ongoing battles with the powers that be at the college.
He regarded my self-taught, southern-poor-boy-turned-
aspirational-bourgeois father with interest, no doubt seeing
glimmers of his own life. They shared an affection for telling tales and creating stories, and I remember my horror
when at one Sunday dinner, Sam calmly told my father that
he "would lie if the truth were in my favor just to keep in
practice!" My father was shocked and taken aback at Sam's
audacity but simply nodded and, after some discussion,
agreed: indeed, they had both re-created the narratives of
their lives, and my father's adolescent desires had become
his adult truths in much the same way that Sam's had his. A
tenuous truce was established, and my folks came to regard
us as a couple as well as joining us from time to time at the
opera or sitting down to hear Mabel Mercer at the St. Regis
Hotel. My mother occasionally joined the crowd at Horatio Street. They were trying to be modern parents and keep
up with the progressive and permissive times and made no
mention of weddings or commitments. And so it went for a
while.

It was not always about friends and the famous. Sam also had moments when the doors to Club 81 were firmly shut to the world. Like many apparent extroverts and indeed like his best friend, Baldwin, he was a deeply private person and required his downtime to think and renew his energy. In these moments, he would also write, and when he returned to the world recharged, he would occasionally bring a page out of the drawer in his coffee table to read the precious paragraphs that he'd crafted. Writing was not something that came easily for him. It was agonizing, but the results were memorable.

He had that kind of eye and that ability to transmute the detritus of everyday living into wordsmith's gold. But the paragraphs were few and far between, and for the most part, he'd disappear into his own world—sit and sip scotch and listen to the music he adored: Maceo Woods's growling organ playing old-school gospel songs like "Peace Be Still," deep-moaning blues that talked of loss and longing, or full-blast operas to which he would sing along. Christmas was a no-fly zone for friends. Club 81 was always closed for the holiday. Sam remained sequestered and meditated on things while surrounding himself with the plangent voice of Bessie Smith. And so the year went by with the unfurling of events and my increasing acceptance by Sam's crowd.

Chapter Two

AND THE BABY MADE THREE

If the red-brick buildings of the West Village were where much of this story plays out, it begins earlier in the quiet, tree-lined streets of St. Albans, Queens, for it was there that I grew up in the aspirational world that was the Black middle-class life of the period. (A wiser, older friend once told me that there was no real Black middle class: our standards and aspirations were always upper class. We may have had middle incomes, but our goals and desires were rarely middle class.) My parents could have been poster children for movin' on up. But unlike the television Jeffersons, it was no situation comedy with canned laughter, but a daily push for acceptance and upward movement.

When I try to think of what attracted Sam to me, I don't look at my photographs (when I do, I'm surprised to find that I wasn't bad looking, and I had a youthful freshness and a direct, fearless gaze). I do look at my upbringing and my education. My mother once told me that I'd been taken to nursery school in a limousine. I certainly hope that the tale is apocryphal, but suspect it is not and know that whatever the truth of it is, the statement sums up the dreams that my parents had for their only child. I'm the product of two people who were the strivers in their families.

My father, Jesse Brown Harris, came from hardscrabble, dirt-poor folks in Napier, Tennessee, and moved north with his mother and two younger siblings in the Great Migration of the 1930s. His older half-brothers had come first, and when they'd acquired a foothold, they brought their mother and the younger family members. Six foot four feet tall at a time when that was very tall, slender, ebony black, and ramrod straight, he was handsome with looks that transcended race at a time when little else did. When he entered a room, people wanted to know who he was. He walked through life with his head held high in what many assumed was arrogance but was in fact a mask for myriad insecurities too numerous to note. His father had been, among other things, a rag-and-bones man who did everything he could to keep the wolf away from his brood in the dark days of the Depression. The letters that my grandmother kept reveal a caring father who, while away in Birmingham, Alabama, trying to keep his family together by working in the steel mills, worried about his progeny and his wife. They are poignant.

Addressed to my father, his eldest son, they reveal anxieties about his family in New York and are filled with promises of sending one dollar in the next letter so that my father could take his mother to the clinic for medical help, and heartfelt apologies for not being able to send more.

Yet despite his impoverished childhood, my father always had a sense of beauty and of self. His aesthetic sense led him to walk across Brooklyn to attend Erasmus Hall High School because he felt it looked like a school should look. The trade-off was that he had to enroll for a general diploma that held him back from higher learning. (There are two Black students in his graduation picture; the other one, Scovill Richardson, light of skin and straight of hair, is barely discernible in the photograph. In one of fate's ironies, his daughter and I would take classes together at NYU decades later.) Never defeated, he took college night courses for most of my childhood; threatened me with Heathcliff, not the bogeyman; and read Pushkin and psychology texts for pleasure. He instilled in me the need to read voraciously and gifted me with his memory, which was able to call up any fact that he'd read or heard in detail when it was necessary, and sent me to the very best schools in the country.

He was a self-taught student of human nature, with a finely tuned awareness of social ironies and a wicked sense of humor that would at times make him literally fall on the floor with laughter. When my college application asked for my grandfather's occupation, he had only a second's hesitation and then, no doubt thinking of all of those letters from Birmingham, wrote in the blank "metallurgist"! We all cackled wildly about that one. "Daddy," as he always signed his letters, wasn't a numbers runner or a player or an absentee father; he wasn't a doctor or a lawyer. He was a constant presence, a rock of stability who said grace before every meal, got down on his knees to pray each night before retiring, and marched us off to Westminster Presbyterian Church each Sunday. The one love of his life beyond learning was his wife, my mother.

While my father was from the hardscrabble South, my mother, Rhoda Alease Jones Harris, was a northern girl; she'd been born in Elizabeth, New Jersey, and grew up in Plainfield, where her father was a Baptist minister. His position meant that her family was respected in the community. Her mother had gone to a women's seminary at the end of the nineteenth century, and her father had trained in theology. They'd met and married, but then slipped up and had too many children, and what would have been idyllic with two or three children on a minister's salary got increasingly difficult as the babies kept coming. I'm sure I'm an only child because my mother was one of ten.

She was petite, light-skinned, smart, and had position in the community that my father much admired, as well as an associate of arts degree in home economics that afforded her diverse job possibilities. She'd worked as the dietitian for the Huntington Hartford family, but left that job as her friends and family kept reminding her it was too much like being a maid. She'd been the dietitian at Bennett College in North Carolina, but found the southern social codes too restrictive and finally found her niche in college administration as a secretary and eventually as an administrator.

They were a fantastic couple: a perfect yang-yin pairing in which one individual dreams big—way beyond the normal—and the other has the financial chutzpah to make it come together and work. Daddy was the dreamer. The poverty of his upbringing was the driving force behind his wanting to get out, and his reading had given him the world to aspire to. Mommy was the pragmatist who could move the world if she could find a place to put her fulcrum. She could rob Peter to pay Paul with the best of them and always come out just fine in the end. Together they were unbeatable at a time when aspirations could become realities if one planned. Plan they did and when, after nine years of marriage, they had me, their only child, they had a raison d'être. Their life became about me, and the energy of the family was centered on we three. As their much-loved only child, I was their major chess piece on the board game that was the American dream, although none of us would have put it that crassly at the time. My success represented their achievement and so it was essential that I be offered every perceived key to success and every opportunity to succeed. There were piano lessons and dance recitals and etiquette classes and very, very good schools.

To be fair, it wasn't all aspiration and pragmatism. There was also fun and a fair dose of bohemian madness. My mother had a talent for decorating and entertaining. One year, she wallpapered one wall of our living room a pattern of chartreuse, black, and silver no less and added chartreuse bouclé drapes; it was arresting, and it worked. She gave parties with unusual themes to which her friends all flocked. They arrived at ten in the evening for dessert and drinks and to watch the night-blooming cereus unfurl its once-a-year petals and then wilt as the dawn approached. Another time, she had them come dressed as babies and answered the door in her own homemade Dr. Denton pajamas complete with feet and drop seat. There was the Belafonte-era calypso party with a bartender serving rum punches and a hired calypsonian who sang risqué songs that I was too young to understand; the cabaret in the finished basement with candles in chianti bottles and checked tablecloths; and the twenty-fifth wedding anniversary party where dry ice provided smoke underneath the punch bowl and burned a hole in the tablecloth. I watched them all from my perch on the landing halfway up and halfway down the steps until it was time to go to bed and listen to the gaiety from my bedroom. My father had an artistic bent as well; he had taken art classes at Pratt and was fairly talented at charcoal and watercolor, but he left the entertaining to Mommy and devoted himself to living his motto, "Big as any of 'em," and caring for we three.

Their friends were artists and academics, doctors, lawyers, undertakers, and other striving government workers, and we hovered on the edge of a crowd of folk who were the outer ring of New York's Black elite, the suburbs of "Negroland." They went to church on Sunday, were not afraid to have a drink or two on Saturday night, and knew how to have and to give others a good time. So I was born into a house with a chartreuse wall, grew up in one hung with paintings from artist friends, and socialized with the children of the same doctors and lawyers and educators and government workers and postmen and middle managers and small-business owners.

That was the day-to-day, but education was the key: the way up the ladder to success. As their only child and the vessel into which they poured all of their aspirational desires, I had to have what they perceived of as the best. The nursery school in question and the limousine were only the beginning. It would ramp up seriously with my next school, which would mold me and influence me for the rest of my life: the United Nations International School.

• • •

The United Nations International School combined my father's aspirations and my mother's practicality. It was in Parkway Village on the way to my mother's job at Queens College, and she organized after-school childcare with a classmate's mother who had been recently widowed. The school had been formally organized only a few years prior, and each year there was talk of moving to a "new school" as the fledgling institution added another grade to stretch for the needs of the original class that was two grades ahead of me. UNIS, as the school became known, was my home away from home for the next ten years of my life.

UNIS became the crucible in which I was forged. My classmates in what was essentially an experiment in international understanding were the children of mid- to upper-level diplomats. They went on home leave every other summer and returned with tales of traveling on the *Queen Mary* and *Queen Elizabeth I*, and I began to dream and push my parents into an even wider world than that of our Queens house. My school friends told tales of Calcutta and Cairo and London and Paris at birthday parties. At their homes, I sat on the floor and watched *The World of Apu* by Satyajit Ray and Danny Kaye in *Hans Christian Andersen* flickering on rented screens. I sang "Frère Jacques" along with "Oranges and Lemons." I ate curries and goulashes and steak and kidney pies, as well as the 1950s-era well-balanced foods that my former dietitian mother cooked:

meatloaf, salmon croquettes, lamb stew, and the occasional newfangled turkey TV dinner as a treat. My friends were named Shikha and Danuta and Eluned, as well as Jennifer and Susan and Charles and Ruth. In the beginning, I was the only Black person in my class and one of the few in the school, along with Nobel Peace Prize winner Ralph Bunche's son in a grade above me. That didn't seem to matter to anyone and certainly not to me. What bothered me more was that I was an American in a world where other cultures seemed so much more exotic and to have a deeper and older history. UNIS began my search for a place in the world and left me with a sense of being a permanent outsider: neither fish nor fowl. But it gave me a fluency in the French language, a lifelong love of French culture, and a general cultural fluidity that amazes others and has stood me in good stead ever since.

It wasn't all aspiration; my paternal grandmother lived in the South Jamaica projects and went to a happy-clappy/holy roller church. Daddy insisted that I spend some time with her as well, and I grew up also knowing the sound shoes made as they galloped up the metal treads of the cement steps and what it's like to be in a hallway where you can smell everyone's dinner and recognize your own, and go to a church where the Sunday rejoicing can take you on a journey. My grandmother was grand fun but basic: children should play with other children. She insisted that I go downstairs and outside to the playground, where the other kids and I looked at one another as though we came from alien planets. In fact, we did. I didn't understand them, and they certainly didn't understand me with my books and my French songs and English rhymes any more than if I'd dropped from the moon. But we tried to bond, over Grandma's Kool-Aid with lemons cut up in it, and I learned that if the cement barrels didn't smell too much like pee, they were a cool place to sit and hide with a book during the hot summer. I adjusted and learned to function there as well.

My checkered academic career then followed a pendulum swing of schools determined by whether I could align my parents with my desires or at least get one of them as an ally. The next battle I won: it allowed me to bypass Brooklyn's Packer Collegiate Institute or a similar ritzy East Side private school and go to the public High School of Performing Arts of *Fame* fame. From the cloistered halls of UNIS, where girls spent time with other girls and guys did Lord knows what, it was on to 120 West Forty-sixth Street, on the subway no less, and a total immersion baptism into the world of the arts.

PA, as we affectionately called Performing Arts, was my goal. I went long before the film *Fame* appeared and had to convince my parents that what had not too many years prior been Metropolitan Vocational High School (*vocational* being a term that raised high anxiety levels in my father) would allow me to go to a good four-year college. There was never any question about that. I'd always known that I had a theatrical bent, I was always front and center in the pageants and recitals at UNIS, and PA would allow me to indulge my dreams of becoming an actress. Entry to Performing Arts was based on audition, and so I worked and crafted audition pieces for all three departments: music, dance, and drama. I was determined to get in. The music part wasn't difficult; I'd had years of piano lessons and had been accepted to the High School of Music and Arts. I made the second set of auditions. Dance and drama were more challenging. I'd had dance lessons but had long since given them up. But no worries: my mother sewed a black sock into the crotch of my outgrown leotard and off I went, twisting and gyrating to music that I've mercifully forgotten. Didn't make it there. For the drama audition, I concocted an audition piece, a monologue from a play that we'd done at UNIS, though the small problem was that I'd played the emperor of China. I went into the room in front of the audition panel, reeled off my monologue, which began, "The emperor of China is Chinese," and answered their questions. Somehow someone saw something. Talent? A glimmer of presence? Who knows? I was accepted into the drama department, skipping ninth grade and entering high school at age thirteen. When in sophomore biology class I sat next to a young man sporting full Cleopatra-style turquoise eye makeup, I knew that my UNIS days had ended.

High school was a bohemian interlude after the European curricular stringencies of UNIS. We had academics for half the day and classes like voice and diction, dance, makeup, and scene preparation for the other half. It was immediately determined that I would never be an ingenue; I was too tall and had too deep a voice and too large a personality to be meek and mild or cute and cuddly. Instead I was the nurse in *Romeo and Juliet*, Catherine Creek in *The Grass Harp*, and the mother in *Raisin in the Sun*, all interesting casting for one who was a scant sixteen at graduation. My UNIS academics stood me in good stead, so I concentrated on the theater courses and on not getting sent back to Andrew Jackson, my local high school, at the twice-yearly project time. As senior year approached, it became time to think of colleges. I was not going to get my way twice, and so colleges that offered a theater major were off the list drawn up by my father.

Before we got into the round of college applications and visits, we took the summer off and finally made the trip to Europe that I'd dreamed about since hearing the tales of their trips from my UNIS classmates. It was the summer of 1963. My parents had decided that it was time for the

Harris family to take the Grand Tour. In the early 1960s, that trip to Europe was, even for Black families, a home-going adventure. *Roots* had yet to Africanize us all. This was particularly true for bourgeois folks like mine for whom Europe was considered the epicenter of culture. We'd tried to go once before, but my father spotted an ad for a place on Martha's Vineyard, and my mother used the deposit for what would have been an early voyage of the SS *France* for the down payment, which allowed us to become summer-home owners, placing us yet another step up the social ladder. This time it was for real. Our month-long trip would celebrate my parents' twenty-fifth wedding anniversary and my sixteenth birthday. Both occurred the following year, but as that summer would precede my college freshman year, 1963 was the time.

We were doing it right with a transatlantic crossing by ship. (Little did we think of the irony of that one.) Arrangements had been made for passage and our cabin booked. The crossing on the German TS *Bremen* was the full megillah: the covered gangway and departure from a pier in Manhattan complete with streamers and confetti, foghorns blowing, tugboats, and the Statue of Liberty disappearing behind us. The clocks changed one hour every day to slowly acclimatize us to the time changes, and a heaping bounty of food was served five times a day: breakfast, lunch, tea, dinner, and midnight snacks. It was deck chairs, bouillon, stewards, and more. And we easily settled into a companionable routine. Then it was London (this was, after all, the Grand Tour). We saw the queen's coach entering the stables from out hotel room window and journeyed to Saffron Walden, a small market town, to meet a friend from UNIS who was in boarding school there . . . and then it was PARIS!

Paris, *la ville lumière*, was a major moment for me. UNIS had given me a native command of French, as well as a lifelong case of galloping Francophilia. The European trip was one that I'd been waiting for since my first trip to the observation deck at Idlewild Airport at age five. I'd vowed then to bring a suitcase on my next visit, naively thinking that was all that was necessary for travel. Our trip was transformational, and I was finally in the Europe spoken of by my classmates. I'd finally made it: I was in France!

We had arrived in Paris, the international capital of all things elegant and luxurious. My father seemed to little notice and care even less. *Europe on Five Dollars a Day* firmly clutched in hand, he indulged his lifelong love for real estate and his nosiness and desire to peek in at the lives of others. He forced-marched us Right Bank, Left Bank, and all around the town on a tour of the city's small, inexpensive hotels. For what seemed like hours, my mother and I dutifully followed the newly purchased green canvas bag he'd slung over his shoulders. Finally, he'd settled on a place near the Place de la République in the oh-so-unchic, off-the-beaten-path eleventh arrondissement that smelled of furniture polish and disinfectant. We thoroughly examined the hotel, met the proprietress (an overworked lady named Elizabeth who spent her days doing the polishing and scrubbing that gave the place its distinctive fragrance), checked in, unpacked our too-large suitcases, stowed the toilet paper that we'd been told was essential for our enjoyment of the trip, and headed out to explore.

The Eiffel Tower, Notre Dame, and the Champs Elysées were miles away in more touristic parts of the city and we'd see them later on our *Five Dollars a Day*–recommended Cityrama tour. However, on our first evening in the City of Light, we strolled down streets of our community entranced by signs that cemented the neighborhood feel of the arrondissement. The butcher, the baker, and the breadmaker's shops all brought back the French lessons that I'd taken since first grade (*le boucher, le patissier, le boulanger*).

The Place de la République was one of the centers of the *quartiers populaires*—the Parisian neighborhoods that were home to many of the working-class Parisians who kept the city flowing. In the 1960s, it remained thoroughly proletarian. The buildings were gray with grime; the work to clean them up had been initiated in 1962 and not yet made its way to this section of town. I vividly remember watching the cafés and brasseries that surrounded the Place de la République, intrigued by the liveliness of the street life. The trip that would mark the coming of age of my oh-so-nuclear family: our discoveries about ourselves, our familial relationships, and the Europe that we'd explored together. I was becoming my own person.

That fall it was back to school, but with all of the intensity of senior year and college looming large on the horizon, it was time to get serious. My father virtually committed *Lovejoy's College Guide* to memory and could spout school statistics as fluently as other men reeled off batting averages. I wanted to go to Sarah Lawrence and major in theater; however, it was Bryn Mawr, which decidedly had no theater major. As they had with his own high school, aesthetics played a role. No other school I visited could match the beauty of Bryn Mawr: the gothic-style stone buildings, archways, cloisters, and towers. In spring it was breathtakingly beautiful with flowering trees and rolling greens, and the academic pedigree was unbeatable. The small glitch was that they were said to require Latin as a part of their entry requirements. I certainly had taken Latin, but at UNIS. No matter, my determined mother marched into the guidance office, found a way to enter that on my transcript, and voilà: the next September, I was sitting in the auditorium listening to President Katharine McBride tell entering freshmen and their families that when they graduated, Bryn Mawr girls could write about anything. I certainly couldn't then and was a less-than-stellar student, squeaking along in everything except French, which I majored in. I did excel in making friends and in fitting in, and unlike many of the other scholarship members of my class, Black and White, amazed my classmates from far more patrician backgrounds with my knowledge of and participation in social matters ranging from private schools (UNIS) to cotillions (I was "presented to society" by the New York Girlfriends at the Waldorf Astoria in New York my freshman year) to summer addresses (that house on Martha's Vineyard). I even managed to circumvent things slightly and discovered a way to participate in college theater. As a French major, I took a junior year abroad, *mirabile visu* with Sarah Lawrence, which had been my first choice for college.

The class of 1968 was a pivot class. The Bryn Mawr that we entered harkened back to an earlier time and was a genteel white institution in which Black maids and porters served meals at table and sang spirituals at Christmastime in the dining halls. It was a school where academic gowns were worn to freshman convocation and a tea set was a requirement listed in the freshmen handbook. There were hall porters who led students back to dorms with lanterns after dark and sign-out books and something called *in loco parentis*. But when I entered in the fall of 1964, the world was changing. Skirts and fists were going up, politics were front and center, and a new world order was emerging. We came clean for Gene (McCarthy); I manned phone banks. We protested against the war in Vietnam, and I led the chorus: "Hey, hey, LBJ! How many kids did you kill today!" We started a chapter on campus for the Student Nonviolent Coordinating Committee (SNCC), and when Whitney Young, the head of the Urban League and a fellow classmate's father, became our graduation speaker, we didn't think he was nearly radical enough.

It was a time of upheaval. President Kennedy had been assassinated during my senior year in high school, and my college years were fraught with assassinations: James Chaney, Andrew Goodman, and Michael Schwerner in Philadelphia, Mississippi, in 1964; Malcom X in 1965; Martin Luther King Jr. in April 1968; and just after graduation, Robert Kennedy in June of the same year. In the four years that marked my college career, the civil rights movement made momentous changes in the world that I was about to enter. Other changes had taken place as well, both light and weighty, ranging from the futuristic vision of the 1964 New York World's Fair that gave us "It's a Small World After All!" to the Vietnam War and LBJ. Even my time in France announced the beginning of what would become known simply as *les événements*—the youth revolution of '68. That changed France forever.

I moved through it all. My academic finishing was a graduate year in France, this time in Nancy, a provincial capital that paled next to Paris, where I longed to be. It netted me a *license ès lettres* and cast my Francophilia in cement. When I returned to New York at the end of the summer of 1969, I knew that I had to get a J.O.B. That, too, had been in the plans.

My mother was at Queens College, and she knew about a new program. It was called the SEEK Program—an acronym for Search for Education, Elevation, and Knowledge, with the oh-so-politically-phrased motto "Learn to Struggle/Struggle to Learn." It appealed to my growing sense of revolutionary awareness and had a better-paying full-time lecturer position than the teaching assistantship that had been offered when I graduated from college. Most important, it was a program designed to funnel African American and Hispanic (here read "Puerto Rican") students into the City University system. It had been offered to me before I left for the graduate year in France and had been promised to remain mine during my studies. The director of faculty and curriculum of the burgeoning program was named Sam Floyd.

I returned from my graduate year, started teaching in the fall of 1969, and immediately began to immerse myself in the world of New York City that I was discovering anew after four years away at college and a graduate year abroad. At first, dutiful daughter to the end, I remained at home. But gradually the lure of Manhattan and the bright lights of what folks from the outer boroughs still referred to as "The City" beckoned. It was time to move. Mindful of the commute to the college and perhaps listening to some unknown inner compass, I traced neighborhoods on the subway lines and decided on Greenwich Village, where I was attending classes toward my doctorate at New York University's nascent Tisch School of the Arts in Performance Studies. I knew no one in the Village and had to threaten the landlord with a racial discrimination suit to get a one-bedroom in what my father referred to as an old-line tenement that had just been renovated with an eye to the area's gentrifying. It was a heady time: friends from high school had also returned to the city from their various college sojourns and we reconnected. The Black Arts Movement was growing and the arts were flourishing. Things seemed possible.

The SEEK Program offered challenges. Many of the students were my age, and the "bourgie" girl from Queens that I was didn't sit well with some of my fellow teachers who were more radical. Others, who had come from southern backgrounds and Black colleges, thought I was stuck up. The fact that my academic discipline was French did not make acceptance any quicker, nor did my mother's connections to the college administration; they just made me suspect in their eyes. It was a time of social paranoia, when everyone was constantly being questioned about allegiances and political stance, and the jockeying for position in the program often became exhausting. I kept my head down, worked at teaching, and found solace (and friends) elsewhere.

In Manhattan, where I lived, some of us formed a group dedicated to spreading the word about the Black Arts Movement through writing for a small uptown tabloid, *The Black American*. To say that the paper was unremarkable is gross understatement; its headlines ran along the lines of, "Didn't God Make Titties?" and it had full-page illustrations inside, but it offered us pages in which to write and an audience. I was in charge of the cultural beat, and I would write my book review column or critique the latest show on African art at the Museum of Modern Art (MoMA) and head out on the A train to deliver it to the editorial offices.

My career as a writer began with those trips uptown. After a few months, I discovered that I was the only one in the group still writing. I knew that I wanted something more, so I rounded up my numerous clips and headed off to peddle my writing wares at a venue that was a tad more legitimate. I began to write for one of the new Black publications that were sprouting up: *Encore American & Worldwide News*. The editor in chief, Ida Lewis, had been the former editor in chief of another new Black publication, *Essence*, but had left and started something more political in tone. I wrote book reviews and did translations of articles from *Jeune Afrique* about international politics and the larger world of the African diaspora, which was beginning to interest me.

My studies at Tisch were culminating, and I had arrived at the stage where I had to propose a topic for my dissertation. I selected the theater of French-speaking West Africa, based on reading a few plays that I'd found on one of my semiannual trips to Paris, because I was fascinated with Senegal's 1966 FESTAC, which celebrated pan-African culture. The preliminary proposal was accepted, and as I went deeper into the topic and took my written and oral exams that would render me A.B.D. (all but dissertation), I realized that there was too much material and so narrowed the topic down to the French-speaking theater of Senegal.

Research necessitated that I make my first trip to Sub-Saharan Africa, which I did in 1972. It was an amazing sensation and as transformational as my initial trip to Paris. A girlfriend who was to accompany me backed out at the last minute, so my mother, always game, signed on, got the shots, and joined me. I'd been to Morocco with my parents. In the early 1970s, after my time in France, they imagined I'd be living in Europe and so had purchased a time-share apartment in the south of Spain, another notch in the aspirational bedpost. (If they'd only shared their thoughts with me, who knows? I might have tried living in Europe.) For a decade, we journeyed there every summer for a few weeks before decamping for a longer stay on the Vineyard. Tangiers was only one hour away from Marbella or two hours from nearby Malaga by ferry. We'd been there several times.

This trip, though, was different. I was going to Black Africa. Looking out of the window as I flew into Dakar's airport was an amazing sight. The plane, which we took from Europe, even felt different; long, lean, ebony-hued folks who looked like my father boarded in flowing garments that I would learn were called *boubous* and they wafted heady smells of incense and pungent perfumes. I was used to understanding languages as I traveled; my French and Spanish stood me in good stead pretty much everywhere I'd ever been except during a month of study in Athens, Greece, where the alphabet had me thoroughly flummoxed. Here, the language was incomprehensible—sibilant and guttural at the same time and completely different from anything I'd ever heard. I was in the motherland: Africa.

When we landed, we headed off to the Hotel de La Croix du Sud, a downtown hotel where Saint-Exupéry had stayed. It was a bastion of white power and privilege designed in what I would come to recognize as French colonial style: high ceilings, wide balconies that let breezes flow, and a decorative style that spoke more of France than of Africa. It mattered not one bit to me: I'd fallen in love with the continent, with Senegal and its handsome, welcoming people, and I'd found a way to combine my love of things French with my growing love of African culture. In Senegal in the early 1970s, I was a curiosity—an African American who spoke fluent French, so someone with whom they could communicate about everything from American politics to R&B music. I made lifelong friends, reveled in the culture, and researched in the archives and libraries. Our trip took us not only to Dakar but farther south to Abidjan, Accra, and Cotonou. This was unusual. Most African Americans headed to English-speaking Ghana and not to the French-speaking countries, and it was five years before Alex Haley's *Roots* would forever transform most African Americans' view of the continent. I was hooked.

I returned to New York and in the fall was back in front of the blackboard teaching students how to conjugate French irregular verbs and trying to reconcile all of my internal contradictions. Although I was very much a child of my time, I was also my parents' daughter. They'd been old parents at age thirty-five, and they'd raised me with their own Edwardian values. I'd been through school; I had a good job. Now it was time to find a husband! I'd dated sparsely in college, little in my graduate year, and not much more in my early years of teaching; I seemed to have no luck in the husband hunt or with men in general. Although it was the permissive 1970s, my love life could have been cast in the 1950s. My first real beau, who dutifully came to Sunday dinners chez Harris and seemed to be a good prospect, turned out to be married—something he'd neglected to mention and, in my naiveté, I'd neglected to ask. That put me off dating and the husband hunt for a while. Subsequent men were either too unsophisticated to fit in with my friends or too political to accept my parents, or maybe I was just too picky. No matter. I soldiered on at the college and enjoyed my single life in the West Village.

It wasn't all doom and gloom. The SEEK Program was a virtual college within a college and offered art and music as well as Yoruba and Swahili. There were instructors from all parts of the globe, and we had a common cause. Benny Andrews taught art; Gail Hightower, music; and Ibrahim Gambari, Yoruba. My colleagues socialized with one another, but I still didn't fit in. Perhaps it was my growing international experience that was at odds with the lifestyles of many of my colleagues who were married and raising families. Perhaps it was my youthfulness: I was a decade younger than most of them and although world traveled, I was significantly less worldly wise—my parents' sheltered daughter.

I did have a growing international awareness and was becoming deeply grounded in European and West African cultures. I'd also continued with my journalistic career. I tried my hand at academic writing, penned an article on Barbara Ann Teer's National Black Theatre for the *Drama Review*, and rapidly discovered that I preferred the world of popular journalism (I liked to get paid for what I wrote) and so continued writing for the new national Black publications like *Encore Worldwide News, Black Enterprise,* and *Essence.* I did interviews with artist Jacob Lawrence, broadcast journalist Gil Noble, and young and upcoming art directors and actresses. I penned occasional travel articles, based on my semiannual European jaunts. I also did book reviews, which is how I found my way to *Essence.* My love of reading and my lifelong habit of reading several books at once made me a natural at book reviews, and so I became the book review editor there.

It was a period when publishers threw book parties and on any given week in the fall or early spring, there were sure to be a few to attend. Doubleday was especially generous, and there were receptions in the Doubleday Suite above the bookstore at the corner of Fifth Avenue and Fifty-third Street, where authors mingled with editors and wine and hors d'oeuvres were plentiful. The gatherings were filled with those that Zora Neale Hurston had baptized the "niggerati" decades earlier, all standing around chatting and being convivial. As the book review editor first at *Encore* and then at *Essence,* I was a regular invitee because Black books were being published. The books and the book parties seemed to indicate just how much progress was being made—at least in getting the word out. All were celebrated with wine at book parties (or scotch at after parties in apartments) and rejoicing. Personal critiques were usually saved and whispered behind closed doors or over the phone the next day.

As an unrepentant book lover, I had taken to making occasional visits to the public relations offices of various book publishers and returning with my fill of books to read and review. Random House and Doubleday were two of my favorite stops. Olivia Blumer at Doubleday aided my guilty pleasure, and I was assured of copies of the books that Doubleday published. In fact, when in 1977 the publisher was coming out with a book that no one knew about, I, who had heard a tape of the author speaking at a librarians' conference, said, to her surprise, that I'd love to interview the author of what they were worried would be a "dud" book. She promised me that if I did, she'd gift me with a case of first editions. I did and she did; the book was *Roots* by Alex Haley.

I have no similar bounty on my bookshelf from Random House, but that building on East Fiftieth Street treated me to an even greater treasure: a fledgling friendship with Toni Morrison. She was still working as an editor at Random House but was clearly an heir apparent to Baldwin's throne. Masked behind her true name, "Chloe" Morrison on the Random House directory in the lobby at 201 East Fiftieth Street, she mentored writers young and old and worked to form the vision of much that is the Black literary canon of the period, introducing writers like Gayl Jones and Henry Dumas, spearheading works by Toni Cade Bambara and Lucille Clifton, and aiding in the publication of works like Rudy Lombard's now-classic *Creole Feast* about the Black chefs of New Orleans. Morrison also created the groundbreaking *Black Book*, which transformed much of how we thought about Black accomplishments and how I personally thought about Black memorabilia. In this, she influenced a generation. She did all of this while working her own word magic and raising two sons.

I can no longer recall the exact moment at which we met, but Morrison was kind, and eventually we began to have occasional lunches at the Italian restaurant downstairs from Random House. Over the lasagna and red wine, I slowly began to think of her as an unspoken big sister/semimentor (although the eternal quest for such and indeed the use of the word was not as commonplace as today).

In my role as a feature writer for *Essence* magazine, I interviewed her in 1976 after the publication of *Sula* and wrote:

It is paradoxical that Toni Morrison who at Random House edits and nurtures the works of such authors as Toni Cade Bambara, Muhammad Ali, Angela Davis, and Lucille Clifton then goes upstairs to Alfred Knopf and has her own work edited. The biography that appears at the back of Ms. Morrison's most recent book is brief and not at all revelatory. It informs readers that Toni Morrison was born in Lorain, Ohio, graduated from Howard University, and received her master's from Cornell. *Sula*, it adds, is her second novel following *The Bluest Eye* and states that Toni Morrison has been a frequent contributor in *The New York Times*. We're told that she taught English and the humanities at Texas Southern University and Howard for nine years. This biography closes with the fact that Ms. Morrison has two sons.

To anyone who has met Toni Morrison the inadequacy of this biography is laughable for she is much more than that. She is one of the most respected black women writers in the literary world and her novels *The Bluest Eye* and *Sula* have become contemporary classics.

I vividly recall sitting in her office looking out at the world of New York skyscrapers through a veil of green plants, yet being surrounded by book-lined walls that reminded of the office's true purpose. I said about it then that it was "both restful and functional" and "the office of a woman whose five senses are always at work." The conversation was wide ranging and described many of Morrison's feelings about not only the authors whose careers she guided, but also her own relationships with them as editor and mentor. We talked about her writing process and the relationships that editors have with their writers. We talked about Black writers with White editors and whether race played a part in the editorial process (she felt not) and the need to avoid the media madness that can affect writers. (This was in the days of book tours and long before self-promotion became a national art.) We talked about her life as a single mother raising two boys and about the need for humor as a balance in life.

I have emblazoned on my brain her description of worrying with the opening sentence to *Sula* and finally settling on blackberries and brambles to represent the sweetness and pain of the life of the Bottom that was being torn down to build the golf course. Her careful parsing of each word and rigorous self-editing were impressive for a fledgling wordsmith. She spoke of the need to express something cogently in ninety words, not nine hundred, and proudly stated, "I realized in the process of writing *The Bluest Eye* that writing had become a compulsion, so I became a writer, that's what I do. I will always be a writer." It was a bold and challenging statement.

The interview was one of my first pieces of feature writing and one of my first outings in the arena of taped interviews and transcripts. I arrived with my cassette tape recorder at the ready, but when I got home, to my great dismay, something had malfunctioned. I don't know if it was my nerves or my inexperience. There was a whole side of the tape that was nothing more than the silent whirring of the machine.

It was a disaster. I have mercifully blanked on the rest of the process; I'm not sure whether I called her back and we revisited some of the ideas or whether I had taken sufficient written notes. Whatever the saving process was, Morrison remained friendly after the publication of the article, and the lunches continued. At one point, she even asked me to read the French translation of *The Bluest Eye* to make sure that they'd gotten the nuances. I was much honored and did so.

By the mid-1970s, I'd added another title to my writing résumé. As the theater critic for the *New York Amsterdam News*, New York's leading Black newspaper, I had two seats on the aisle for the second night of any show opening in New York City. Theater, my first love, was another refuge, and in those years in New York City, it was amazing. There were dramas by David Mamet and works by Miguel Piñero and Ntozake Shange. Joe Papp's Public Theater was sending drama to Broadway. There were also musicals that were redefining the genre, like *Pacific Overtures*, *A Chorus Line*, and *Chicago*, and the Great White Way was blacking up with African American shows from *Raisin* to *The Wiz* to *Dreamgirls* to *Ain't Misbehavin'*. I may have given up acting for writing, but I was there for them all, cheering those trailblazers who had more gumption than I did.

I've always loved music as well, all types of music, and boasted a collection of records that included not only the

Motown and R&B hits that would have been expected, but a catalogue of vinyl that expressed my wide-ranging tastes, from the *Missa Luba*, a Roman Catholic Mass as practiced in the Congo, to Leontyne Price's operatic selections, and a few Beatles albums tucked away from my Beatlemaniac days in college.

I was a conundrum, a pile of insecurities about not being Black enough or pretty enough or anything enough: too light to be dark and too dark to be light. In those days, color counted, and I had my thick but fine hair whipped up into an Afro and wore aviator glasses in the style of Angela Davis. Inside, I still had the little "bourgie" girl from Queens who wanted desperately to belong with the in crowd—who was at odds with the socially aware SEEK Program teacher who wanted to fit in with colleagues, and who was dueling with the newly emerging international sophisticate. I also wanted to find that "other"—the man who was supposed to, if not take me away from all of this, be a partner, as my parents were. Somewhere there was supposed to be someone with whom I could build and grow and move on to the next level. (My loving Edwardian parents had read me all of those "happy ending" fairy tales.) He clearly wasn't on the Vineyard; there I never really fit in with the doctors' and dentists' offspring who barely tolerated my bluestocking tendencies. (I read too much and didn't really do the beach and nighttime party scene. My summers were marked by books and fudge from Darling's candy store.) Prospects in the Village and on the West Side where I hung out with my friends didn't look good: too many married men, and I'd already fallen for that once. Queens College hadn't offered much either. Then one day, I must have left for the bus stop shortly after Sam Floyd, the colleague my mother had stalked to ensure that I had my job. That timing changed my life forever.

Mommy's Sunday Roast Chicken

The southern tradition of chicken on Sunday was often respected at my house when I was growing up. It was usually either fried or roasted. My mother, the former dietitian, made sure that however it was served, it was accompanied by at least two vegetables and a salad. (Back then, that meant iceberg lettuce with a few cottony tomatoes and a slice of onion.) Fried chicken was my childhood favorite, but as I got older, I began to appreciate the virtues of a good roast chicken, and it was one of the first dishes I mastered when I moved out on my own. It's still one on which I pride myself and judge other cooks.

– Serves six –

1 chicken (3½ to 4 pounds)
4 tablespoons butter
2 tablespoons olive oil
1½ tablespoons Bell's Poultry
  Seasoning

2 teaspoons finely ground sea
  salt
½ teaspoon finely ground black
  pepper
1 medium onion, peeled

Preheat the oven to 450°F. Remove the bag of giblets from the cavity of the chicken and wash the bird thoroughly inside and out. Pat dry.

Place half the butter in a small saucepan and melt it. Add the olive oil. Cut the remaining butter into small pieces and insert it under the breast and leg skin of the chicken.

Mix the poultry seasoning, sea salt, and pepper together in a small bowl. Roll the onion in the butter and oil and then roll it in the seasoning mixture and place it in the cavity of the chicken. Pour the remaining butter over the chicken and rub the remaining seasonings into it.

Place the chicken in a roasting pan in the preheated oven. After 15 minutes, lower the heat to 350°F and roast, checking occasionally, for 1 hour and 15 minutes, or until the chicken juices run clear when pricked with a fork at the leg joint. Serve hot.

Chapter Three

BANTAM SAM WAS *THE MAN*

Samuel Clemens Floyd III had been right in front of me at the SEEK Program from my first days there. His story began fifteen years earlier than mine and more than five hundred miles away in the South at the height of the Depression in 1933. He was the youngest of four children born to Samuel Floyd and his wife, Zula, in Durham, North Carolina. Like all other southern cities of the period, Durham was segregated; Blacks lived in the south and southeastern quadrants of the city in an area known as Little Hayti (pronounced Hay-tie in an erudite if mispronounced reference to the hemisphere's first Black republic). But Durham was different. From the turn of the twentieth century onward, Durham had a unique place in the history of Black America because it was, in the words of no less than W.E.B. DuBois, "the business Mecca of the South." He proclaimed, "There is in this small city a group of five thousand or more colored people whose social and economic development is perhaps more striking than that of any similar group in the nation." Durham and its role as an incubator for Black success was so striking that it is one of the few things that DuBois and Booker T. Washington could agree on, with Washington adding that the race relations were cordial and evidenced "the sanest attitude [among] white people toward the blacks."

Durham's special position as a southern Black bastion of aspiration and attainment meant that the city had long been an incubator for business. North Carolina Mutual Life Insurance Company, the epicenter of Durham's business community, was the largest Black-owned business in the United States, and its founders, with names like Merrick, Moore, and Spaulding, were those at the pinnacle of Durham's Black social hierarchy. North Carolina Mutual and other similar businesses spawned a middle class and even an upper class that created a rich cultural life that defined the city. Parrish Street, Black Durham's main drag, boasted a section of Black-owned banks, insurance companies, and other businesses. There were a Black-owned hotel, two theaters, and numerous restaurants, clothing stores, and other businesses. It was known as the Black Wall Street.

Not only was Durham a town that was filled with thriving Black businesses (although they certainly felt the pinch of the Depression), it was also a town that boasted one of the country's few tax-supported Black institutions of higher learning: North Carolina College for Negroes (now North Carolina Central University). Established in 1910, it was a thriving academic center and another cultural hub in the city. Social success in the town was marked by the distance between the railroad tracks and the college, and the Floyd household was closer to the railroad tracks and farther down from North Carolina Central than Sam probably would have liked. It was certainly not on Fayetteville Street, where the Spauldings and the Moores lived, but it was pleasant and it was home.

By his own account, Sam had an ordinary childhood attending local parties given in private homes and indulging in the myriad activities that the community provided for its youth. His older sisters, Shirley and Bernice, had preceded him into high school, and, as some of the most beautiful girls in Durham with their copper skin and their light eyes, had garnered more than their fair share of beaus. Younger brother Sam dutifully chaperoned, tagging along and basking in their glow. Many years later, when maundering in his cups, he'd moan about the opportunities dashed by an early, unmarried pregnancy of one of them. (I've long forgotten which sister.) He made sure that his sister got her prenatal exercise by walking her up and down the railroad tracks and recounted how he'd loved her fiercely and unreservedly, but the experience particularized him and set him off from others in a way that he didn't like and would never forget.

Sam attended North Carolina College and majored in English and later became a teaching assistant there. He somehow made his way to New York as an English major and fledgling writer. He ended up in the Village and in the same apartment building as James Baldwin, with whom he became friends, and had a variety of jobs, including being one of the first Black writers at *Newsweek* magazine. By the late 1960s, though, he'd returned to academe and become the director of faculty and curriculum at the fledgling SEEK Program at Queens College.

The church was in his blood. He used to joke about his mother's father, a minister, who fathered eighteen children. "Like a golf course!" he'd whoop. His mother was, as he put it, in the "back nine" among the younger children. So was his uncle William Taylor, who lived with them in Durham. He attended the deeply historic White Rock Baptist Church, where musicologist and slave song expert Miles Mark Fisher was the pastor, and Sam's musical talents allowed him to make some extra cash playing the organ for St. Titus Episcopal Church.

I wasn't any better at asking questions of Sam than I had been of my first beau, so much of Sam's life before I met him remained a mystery to me. I gleaned information about it from observation and from meeting his friends in all walks of life and overheard snippets of conversation or from his repeated waves of remembrances after too much J&B. My deepest knowledge of him and his background came from the trip that we made together to Durham, where he introduced me to his mother and some of his childhood friends.

Durham was an adventure. The tree-shaded front porch of his mother's Craftsman bungalow reminded me of the one in which my maternal grandmother lived, and his friends the Warrens seemed like some of my distant relatives, with lifestyles and manners that were familiar. Elizabeth Ann, the daughter of the family, was about my age, and we remained in touch for a good while. Sam clearly deemed me presentable and suitable as a potential life's companion. I was taken around to meet the friends of his aspirational youth. He took me for tea with his favorite teacher. When she, with the exacting precision of an old-school English professor, informed us over the fine china cups of Earl Grey tea that she'd been to the dentist for some prophylaxis, I called on my Bryn Mawr–honed social skills and did not giggle or guffaw. Durham presented another side of Sam, one that was far removed from the sophistication of his New York persona and revealed that there was yet another valent to his personality. Sam revered Durham as home and as the place that had formed him, and he dearly loved it.

But even in Durham, Sam had his haunts and his hiding spots. One night, after a day of fine Durham propriety, he revealed some of that. He decided that we should head off to Minnie Hester's, an after-hours joint that was located in someone's kitchen and was clearly illegal. The only picture I have of the two of us together shows us sitting at a table, lips greasy with barbecue and surrounded by glasses that contained my first taste of white lightning. We're both grinning like Cheshire cats and savoring the moment. I'm looking besotted with drink and with Sam, and he's looking cat-that-got-the-cream-pleased that he had conquered a Durham that had wounded him in some unspoken way as a child. Little did I know that my trip to Durham had been a true gift; it gave me another Sam, a view of him that few others saw, a side he shared with none of his college colleagues or his famous friends.

By the time I met him, Samuel Clemens Floyd III was a subtly captivating man in his early forties with smooth copper skin (Angelou's black golden amber) and silky dark brown hair frothed into what my mother called an egg-beater Afro. Brown eyes that twinkled with mischievous glee and a bewitching smile made him quite handsome, and he had an aura that filled the room wherever he went. The Elizabethans would have described his temper as choleric: his fits of temperament could be excoriating, yet they would pass like a southern squall and his choir-boy-with-a-secret smile charmed everyone back. He was as pugnacious as a young James Cagney and left more than one restaurant in a huff after some slight real or imagined, threatening to turn over the tables and shoot the owners, but when he sat stroking Blues in the apartment/sanctuary that he had created for himself, he was at peace, and none of this was apparent.

He had just enough magnolia and honeysuckle in his mouth to charm the world, and his conversation dripped with witty southernisms like sorghum syrup on a biscuit. Listening and watching, I could hear the country boy from Durham, North Carolina, in his speech and see it in the old-style gold-rimmed crown on one of his front teeth until he had it removed. But Sam was big-city dapper in his dress with tailored suits that made him "sharp as a rat's turd," he would crow gleefully in one of the southernisms he cultivated.

He wasn't tall or flashy, but he commanded any room he entered simply by crossing the threshold. This was his gift and his curse, for it made him catnip for any woman who had half a gram of estrogen. He attracted women unconsciously. He was a bantam rooster—a cock of the walk—who was clearly aware of and reveled in his position. He would, on occasion, crow about a litany of the famous and the near famous who had been his paramours. He'd recount how Diana Sands had fallen under his sway and he'd squired Maya Angelou around and was friends with Nina Simone, and more. The folks he could summon with a telephone call ranged from educators to media stars. How this rare bird ended up at the SEEK Program in Queens College was a mystery, but one for which we were all thankful.

I got to know him better and better as our friendship grew, but Sam remained to me and to most other folks who knew him a bit of a cipher. He wasn't secretive or silent. Quite the contrary; he had no problem with reminding folks about whom he knew and what he had done. The term *walker* had not yet been created to define men whose role is to dress up and squire certain women about town. Sam's qualities as an eloquent and attractive man who could hang upscale, downtown, or even down home with the best of them made him a much-coveted escort among the ladies of his circle of friends. He responded with his usual flair and finesse, squiring them to openings and book parties, operas and theatrical events.

For most of them, Sam was more than a walker. He was a combination of big brother and confidant, lover and man, as in "*My* man." I was certainly too naive and without a sense of belonging in the same club as his famous women friends to question, and I didn't want to risk what were his very real and, to me, very frightening rages that could erupt from nowhere, triggered by a word or a gesture or the remembrance of some past slight. While I reveled in the excitement of the group, I also cowered internally more often than not, never knowing exactly what word or gesture might take the evening from pleasurable to problematic. I never knew just who was who or, for that matter, what was what, but I did know that his ladies always had more than a hint of possessiveness about him that kept me on guard. They cherished his presence and his wit and vied with one another for his friendship like hens circling a prize rooster. I was fifteen to twenty years younger than most of them, green for my age, foolish, and playing waaaay over my weight class.

The ladies paraded and occasionally gave me the side eye, but gradually, I came to understand that being with Sam was being with someone who was a major part of a twentieth-century literary court: that of James Baldwin. Their proximity as neighbors had led to Sam becoming what David Leeming, one of Baldwin's biographers, described as one of Baldwin's "closest and most trusted friends." If Jimmy, as I learned to call Baldwin, was the sun king, the *roi soleil*, around whom the court revolved, Sam was in many ways its master of the revels and depended on by all of the members. No king's fool, Sam; rather, he was a good friend, sensitive to Jimmy's needs, and able to understand the inadvertent sequester that fame places on some lives. He made Jimmy's life with fame easier, told him the truth and argued with him, and treated him like a friend, not an icon. Trusting Sam, Jimmy accepted me without questioning.

Club 81, Sam's small one-bedroom roost, on the parlor floor front, was the frequent locus for encounters and boasted a coveted Village attribute: a fireplace. It was furnished simply in what has been described as professorial disarray, with shelves overflowing with books and papers, a couch, coffee table, dining table, and straight ladder-back armchair with a woven rush seat by the window in which Sam would sit and observe the world. The art was nondescript. A print on the wall over the monastic twin bed in the tiny bedroom and overflowing bookshelves in the entrance and in the living room pretty much took up all of the wall space. One year at Christmas, he did receive a small Beauford Delaney oil painting of a sad clown that he cherished. It was on an easel on a table next to the couch.

Aside from his speech patterns, Sam also retained some of his southern behaviors in his northern space. A lover of golf, no doubt an affection he'd acquired as a child in Durham, caddying as many southern Black boys did to make some extra money, he'd haul his clubs on the subway and play the municipal courses around the city on sunny days or ride the Long Island Rail Road to one of the championship courses nearby. He goaded me into taking golf lessons, playing on my obvious desire to be his "partner" and declaring loudly that no one would ever be Mrs. Sam Floyd who couldn't hit a decent golf ball. I tried. Oh Lord, did I try, but I am so nearsighted that I could never tell where the ball went. I dutifully took my golf lessons and bought golf clubs. (Used!

I wasn't a complete fool.) The upshot was that although he complimented me earnestly on my abilities and encouraged me at every turn, taking me to driving ranges and putting greens, I never really fell in love with the game as he had.

I kept trying. It didn't work with the golf, but I knew that golf wasn't really the problem; we'd connect on other things. I was ready to be molded into something and desperately wanted to be someone's helpmate, to use the old-fashioned Baptist term that my grandmother's minister liked. I wanted to share something with someone and to cultivate that "you and me against the world thing" that I saw in my parents. I was more than willing to make some adaptations for that.

I fared a little better with singing lessons, which he also encouraged me to take. One of his favorite compliments for me was to lean in while I was saying something, smile his devastating smile, and say, "Her voice was ever soft, gentle, and low, an excellent thing in a woman." That line from Act 5, Scene 3 of *King Lear* would always make my liver quiver and undo me. Folks often praised my speaking voice, and several said that I should try singing although I cannot carry a tune in a bucket. But for Sam, I'd give it a try, and so I'd somehow managed to find a used baby grand piano, have it transported to my fourth-floor walk-up, and get it tuned. A protégée of Martina Arroyo—another friend of Sam—was persuaded to give me singing lessons. I'd had voice and diction courses in high school and could project my voice from my diaphragm. At one point, my childhood piano teacher thought I might have perfect pitch, so I do-re-mi'd with the best of them but somehow never could get the hang of that either. The lessons stopped after a few months, but the piano remained for several years until I gave it away to someone who would carry it down those four flights of stairs.

My Galatea period ended with the singing lessons. Sam had better luck with me and alcohol. My parents were not teetotal by any means; they had an occasional whiskey sour or a martini, and our home had a full range of alcoholic beverages that we offered to guests. I'd become a wine aficionado while studying in France but never had developed a taste for brown liquor. (This was in the days before vodka became the rage.) I tried scotch, the preferred tipple of Sam's group, but I couldn't hack it. Bourbon and ginger ale was Sam's suggestion for an adult drink for me, and Jack and ginger (Jack Daniels and ginger ale) seemed to roll off my tongue nicely. Sam also taught me bar etiquette, like how to tent a twenty-dollar bill and place it in front of me on the bar to let the bartender know to run a tab—this in the days of the three-dollar drink. I learned how to scope out a bar and know when it was wiser, and easier on my palate, to order bourbon and ginger ale as opposed to the red wine that was my usual tipple. He schooled me that Jack Daniels was not bourbon but Tennessee sipping whiskey and that too much Old Crow could make you 'shamed (allegedly the reason the crow on the front had his head averted). It's knowledge that still stands me in good stead.

Drinking seemed to be a part of what we did back in the 1970s and 1980s, and drinking outside of someone's house usually meant the hard stuff. Sure, there was wine at folks' homes, usually qualified as either red or white—no grape varietal names or appellations were used. Mercifully, I stayed out of the Cream White Concord and Boone's Farm Apple Wine zone; Fazzi Battaglia Verdicchio was one of the whites that I remember more for its distinctively shaped bottle than for its taste. Usually the wine came in half-gallon jugs. The reds consumed ran to Beaujolais or whatever was in the bin at the local liquor store but were mainly for dinner and brought as hostess gifts. Whites were the only wines considered for bar drinking. There were also the rosés: Mateus and Lancers were hostess gift standbys because they "went with everything" and made one appear a wine maven. I had the added ability of being able to pronounce the wine of choice in French (or faked Italian), thereby conveying a sophistication that was not evidenced by my palate. I could wow my own friends and age-mates with my choices, but with Sam and the crowd from Club 81, I needed all of the props I could get in the alcohol department, where I was something of a laggard and a piker.

For Sam and Jimmy and the others, it was not about wine but about scotch, and lots of it. Johnnie Walker was often the brand of choice, but I remember Sam sitting down on multiple occasions with a beaker of J&B (Justerini and Brooks, I learned, after picking up untold bottles of it at the liquor store on Eighth Avenue on my way to Sam's house). In that crowd, house parties were not really parties but rather gatherings of like-minded friends at someone's home. They were invariably lubricated with these tipples, and more often than not, a meal was part of the evening, whether it was planned for and prepared by the host or hostess, ordered in, or cobbled together in the moment from ingredients in the fridge. At times it seemed that the social life was a combination of Hemingway's moveable feast and a nongambling version of the oldest reliable, permanent floating crap game in New York from *Guys and Dolls*: the venues changed, the participants varied with season and locale, and the food ranged from stellar to so-so, but there was always enough to drink, be it scotch, bourbon, or wine.

Perhaps the most important thing that I learned from Sam, or at least the one that has stood me in best stead, was how to love cooking and to entertain lavishly. Sam fine-tuned my entertaining skills. I'd certainly cut my teeth on my mother's parties of my youth, and I had inherited her flair for the dramatic along with my father's love of spectacle, so I had a lot going for me. Sam, however, cultivated my cooking skills and saddled me for the rest of my life with the shopping habits of a child of the Depression for whom a bare larder was a terrifying thing. (To this day, I shop as though I'm responsible for a hungry family of eight, not a single individual.) Sam's mantras were: *If you can afford it, buy it. Always offer your friends the best that you can and have it in prodigious abundance.* He reinforced things that my parents had demonstrated but would have never thought of saying to their young, and I expect they thought unsullied, daughter. *When you go to someone's home, never call for a particular brand of liquor: ask for scotch or bourbon, not J&B or Maker's Mark. Accept what you're given with grace. Earn your place at the table or in the room by being as entertaining as you can, and if you cannot be your best self wherever you go, stay home.* They were finesses, but they were enduring.

Sam was never happier than when puttering around in the kitchen preparing some elaborate feast that he'd devised in his head. A gourmet and gourmand, he'd plan a menu, shop for the best ingredients, and serve it proudly to friends. One holiday, a roast goose was the challenge that he set for himself, and he brought it off done to a perfect turn. It was a time when the country, and especially New York, was emerging from the chicken potpie and meatloaf aesthetic that had been the 1950s and much of the 1960s at many of our tables. Julia Child and James Beard had unleashed the culinary revolution, and even restaurants had begun to explore not only other cuisines but even culinary history. Restaurant Associates gave us both La Fonda del Sol and the Forum of the

Twelve Caesars. At home, fondue sets graced tables, and cru-
dités complete with a savory dip made from Lipton Onion
Soup were the ne plus ultra in entertaining styles. I cracked
open my *Mastering the Art of French Cooking* and learned how
to make *coq au vin*, although I couldn't find the required pearl
onions at Balducci's and substituted a can of black-eyed peas
that I had on hand. It wasn't classically French, but it made
a tasty meal. I tried my hand at making pâté with a bit more
success and kept on cooking.

So we bonded over cooking and cooked together, and
even though we lived in apartments several blocks apart, it
seemed as though there was one larder and certainly one
set of cooking equipment. Our *batteries de cuisine* cohabited
even if we didn't. My terrine went to live with him, and his
platter resided at my place. We shared recipes and occasionally cookbooks, but in truth we were both intuitive cooks
who worked more from instinct and taste than from recipes.
Sam's kitchen was small and old fashioned, with a porce-
lain sink usually overflowing with dishes, and in New York
fashion, often more than the occasional roach was roam-
ing. My kitchen was not much larger, but it at least had one
appliance that dated post–World War II. It was considerably
cleaner because I am phobic about roaches and about wash-
ing dishes after use and swabbing out every drop of water
left in the sink.

I was in my first apartment, complete with the requisite

Dansk pottery and Pottery Barn glasses, but was developing a collection of fine china and Waterford crystal, and had even hied myself to Tiffany's to buy sterling for one—Hampton pattern—in hopes that it might be the start of my "hope chest." I even had a set of fish knives that I'd picked up in Portobello Road during my junior year, which meant I often served a fish course at a dinner party just to use them. Sam's cutlery was nondescript, his crockery had come straight from the restaurant of a friend, and his glasses were simple, basic, and large enough to hold a good solid drink. But when he set a table, it was lovely, and no one ever invited forgot the feeling of being treated to something extra special.

We were an odd couple—the mature man who was the cynosure of all and the French teacher fifteen years his junior who tagged along almost as an afterthought yet kept up with conversations and was developing a presence of her own. On closer observation, it was not that complicated. I was not someone who had set my hat for Sam; indeed, I was as bewildered as anyone else about why he'd settled on me. That may have been my attraction: I was also young enough and smart enough and malleable enough to be molded in a way that the other women were too mature and self-aware to countenance. Most important, I simply slunk off to my corner and retreated when things got confrontational. My parents never fought in front of me, and as a result, I'd never learned that fighting is part of how a relationship endures and that learning how to fight and how to make up is a big part of being a couple. It was a mystery to me. I simply went into myself, got quiet, got hurt, and mentally licked my wounds, hoping that they would heal before it happened again the next time. I got really good at that.

We shared other things as well: love of language, love of literature, love of Paris, and a sense of respect for and a love of the gentle, mannered ways that defined some lives in the South. Sam knew them from growing up in Durham through the lens of a transplanted southerner; I, from the preserved-in-amber South in which I had been raised in the North.

As we grew as a couple, we shared these loves. Our love of language and literature resulted in long conversations about everything from the denizens of the Harlem Renaissance, whom Sam had known, to chats about the latest books that were coming out. As a book reviewer, I visited publishing offices and left with reviewers' copies and galleys, which we shared and then discussed. His Sunday salons were almost a throwback to the Harlem Renaissance. In 1973, we compared notes on *In Love and Trouble* by Alice Walker and *Sula*, the second book by Toni Morrison, who was becoming a literary colossus. The year 1974 saw Angela Davis's autobiography, Maya Angelou's *Gather Together in My Name*, and

If Beale Street Could Talk, by Baldwin himself. By 1976, there was a tidal wave of work, including Alice Walker's *Meridian* and *Singin' and Swingin' and Gettin' Merry Like Christmas,* the third installment in the Angelou's autobiographical saga. (We both knew the title was the bowdlerized version of Maya's mother's expression "twitchin' and bitchin' and getting merry like Christmas.") Then there was the publishing juggernaut that was *Roots: The Saga of an American Family.* Like my cooking utensils, the galleys and books ended up at Sam's place sooner or later, blending in with our mutual stuff. To my mind, they were the glue that cemented our relationship and the living testimonial of our growing relationship and our growing couplehood.

We were social, oh so very social. We'd go out of an evening. As a theater reviewer, I had two seats for everything that opened on and off Broadway. We saw them all: the good, the bad, and the truly awful. I sat through *1600 Pennsylvania Avenue* and an astonishingly bad *Macbeth,* which, in homage to Orson Wells, was set on a Caribbean island. Each actor had a different, often slipping accent, and Esther Rolle was Lady Macbeth. Sam had an unerring radar for the bad plays and the good sense to demur on these or walk out at intermission. I was still the good kid and felt bad for the actors who would have to return for the second act to an empty house. So we occasionally would meet at Joe Allen's or Frankie and Johnny's or another restaurant after the theater where Sam had spent the second act in the bar while I'd faithfully stayed for the performance.

We certainly shared discussions about our work at Queens College in the SEEK Program, and we shared Paris. While many at SEEK seemed to feel that my love of Paris and ability to speak fluent French made me somehow less than an authentic Black person, Sam seemed to understand and indeed was something of a Francophile himself. He visited frequently, often as a guest of his friend Baldwin. The September 3, 1970, issue of *Jet* magazine, the chronicler of all things Black at that time, has articles on the ongoing search for Angela Davis, an article about Alice Walker whose *The Third Life of Grange Copeland* had just been published, and, in the column "Paris Sketchbook" by Art Simmons, this mention:

Baldwin's spending the summer here vacationing with friends in a fabulous flat in Neuilly, France. Guests at his recent birthday party included Samuel C. Floyd, director of faculty and curriculum development at Queens College in Flushing New York here writing a film script and working on the biography of his grandfather, the Rev. Junius Taylor.

As a friend of Baldwin, he'd often summered with him in both Paris and, later, the South of France. Although we were never in Paris together, we could speak knowledgeably about the clubs, like Le Sept and Le Bilboquet, and restaurants like the Brasserie Lipp and others that we both knew. Despite my love of Paris, I knew that there were racial issues and social divides that mirrored those in the United States, albeit with different Black folks. I'd learned about the racism of former colonials during my junior year, and I certainly didn't envision myself living there full time as an expatriate. But I did love Paris and journeyed there twice a year. Sam too knew that his lot was on the western side of the Atlantic, and although he traveled to France often to visit his friend Jimmy, he never considered making his life there. He did adopt some of the French expressions that I unconsciously used in speech, and I adopted his southernisms and reveled in his eclectic tastes. And so we went on.

Roast Goose

When I think of Sam's cooking, the one dish that comes immediately to mind is the memorable roast goose that he prepared one Christmas. I can admit that I have never and probably at this stage am never going to prepare a roast goose. However, if I should get the notion to do so, I would turn to one of my favorite French cookbooks that I acquired back in the 1970s during my French cooking phase. While Julia Child had recipes that were complex, incredibly detailed, and required many steps, French Cooking for Everyone by Alfred Guérot took a more Gallic approach to directions and assumed that the cook knew something about the kitchen. The recipe for roast goose is a scant paragraph. There is no ingredients list or methodology parsed out in small, easy-to-follow sentences—rather, basic instructions on how to cook the bird. This is my version.

Season, truss, and place the goose on a rack in a shallow roasting pan in a 325°F oven. Roast until the leg joints move freely. While the goose is cooking, periodically spoon off the fat as it accumulates, reserving it for later uses. It will take an oven-ready eight-pound goose about four hours to roast.

Chapter Four

OH, THE PEOPLE YOU'LL MEET!

Once Sam invited someone into his world, he was generous with his friends. At least he was that way with me. We started slowly. I was heading down to spend a week in Haiti with Anna Horsford, a high school friend. I'd been to Haiti once before with my first beau (the one who'd turned out to be married), but this time it was a girlfriend trip. We'd booked a room at the celebrated Hotel Oloffson, feeling that it would make a good roost, and we were going down to have fun in the sun.

Haiti has always been one of those litmus paper destinations: people either love it and view the artistry and the cultural richness, or they hate it and cannot get beyond the poverty that exists. I loved the country: its history and culture and place in the African diaspora. On my return to the island for a second visit, Sam casually said, "You must try to see my friend Rosa Guy; she's down there writing."

The Oloffson, famed as the hostelry that is fictionalized as the center of Graham Greene's *The Comedians*, looked like Hansel and Gretel's gingerbread house designed by Edward Gorey. Had the sun not been shining and the rum not been flowing, the turreted, veranda-bedecked, carpenter-gothic pile might have seemed ominous. This, though, was in the days when Al and Sue Seitz were the innkeepers and the hotel was welcoming, and it was one of the Caribbean's most storied spots. The rooms were basic: whirling ceiling fans, sputtering air-conditioning, creaky beds that were as spavined as the mules that carried visitors up to the Citadel in Cap Haitien, but they were covered with bright fabrics and the walls were adorned with the art that was the country's glory. The rooms were comfortable but certainly nothing to write home about. However, they were not why folks stayed at the Oloffson. It was all about the public spaces: the veranda with its rocking chairs and the bar where all happened. There, it was Haiti's own Rhum Barbancourt all around.

The hotel was every writer's dream, with the flotsam and jetsam of the island circulating at cocktail time. Modern pirates rubbed shoulders with pale-skinned newcomers, their sharp eyes evaluating each summer cotton frock and gold-braceleted arm and calculating schemes and scams. Paint-daubed artists sought solace in the bottom of glasses, weary island-exiled writers fled from the blank page, social-ites fought ennui, and white-suited Aubelin Jolicoeur, the prototype for Greene's character Petit Pierre, hovered: a celebrity in search of an audience. The sophistication was palpable.

Below the veranda that fronted the hotel, a swimming pool beckoned. It was there that I met Rosa Guy (pro-nounced the French way to rhyme with *key*). When I asked about her at the front desk, I was told that she came every day to swim. Soon enough, they pointed her out to me. She'd been swimming laps, exhibiting a svelte figure that was being admired slyly by more than one onlooker. She emerged otter sleek and joined Anna and me at the mahog-any bar for a drink. We later invited her to join us for din-ner at La Lanterne, a restaurant in a private house in the hills of Pétionville above the capital that was run by a Swiss chef and his Haitian wife. There we dined on chicken fla-vored with coconut and pineapple and were served at can-dlelit tables sitting around a swimming pool. We foreswore our Barbancourt cocktails and drank chilled French wines, exchanged pleasant banalities about life in general, and enjoyed the balmy breezes of the tropical night. At the end of the evening, our taxi dropped her off at her home. Actu-ally we dropped her off at a depression in the roadside and I remember watching in amazement as she exited the car, hopped over the embankment, and disappeared down what revealed itself to be a steep flight of steps headed toward her home. I still have a mental picture of her disappearing down a hillock into the night.

We would meet again after she returned to New York, as she was an integral part of Maya and Jimmy's group. Although always ferociously focused on her writing, Rosa was also a great flirt. At times it seemed she was flirting just to keep in practice. She and Maya often had an unspoken but very real competition with leading guys on and with seeing who could pull more men. Rosa, with her lilting Caribbean inflections and her twinkling eyes, often was the winner. The scuttlebutt ran that the men might squire her home but they would rarely spend the night. Rosa would put them out before the morning, as she was always up with the dawn and back at work. Work always came first. No one joked about that.

Rosa's best friend in the group was Louise Meriwether, who was equally ferocious about her writing, but as with many girlfriends, they were in other ways opposites: Louise was not up to Rosa's flirting competition. That's not to say she was a nun or a saint, but rather that she didn't play on the man-go-round that defined the social life of some members of the group. Rosa and Louise were often together, and by the time that I met them, their friendship had muted and melded their personalities somewhat. I was noted for constantly calling one by the other's name, confusing them until they spoke. They tolerated my lapses. In earlier years, that

wasn't an issue. If I didn't know them by face, I
by temperament. Rosa was quicksilver; Louise
times placid, at others turbulent, with the ability
tence to wear down rock.

Perhaps I felt more of an affinity with Louis
a northern-based African American, she mirro
that I knew: a world that spoke to my own roots.
like me, a child of the Great Migration; she ha
in Harlem during the Great Depression. She ki
that connected her to my parents, who were or
older than she. *Daddy Was a Number Runner*, her
published in 1970, was a book about a time and
were familiar to my parents, a world about which
The novel, which was originally published with
by Jimmy, connected with Black folks of all ages.
it with my parents; they got it.

The kinship I felt to Louise probably also
with her occasionally bringing her mother to
events. It made me feel less self-conscious about
with my own mother in tow. My mom reveled in
mian life of Sam's crowd and hungered for the i
stimulation that took her away from the bourged
of Queens, where talk ran to social club doings
luncheons and Sigma Wives formal dances. Ou
"charges" made for an instant rapprochement—
in any case.

Rosa and Louise were friends of Sam's and intimates of Maya's. (In fact, Maya had roomed with Rosa on her arrival in New York.) In my mind, they formed a triumvirate with Paule Marshall, another pivotal member of the group. If Louise and Rosa were accessible, Brooklyn-born Paule Marshall was more of a cipher. Her parents were immigrants from Barbados who'd moved to Brooklyn's Crown Heights neighborhood, and her first book, *Brown Girl, Brownstones*, told of that immigrant experience. She wrote about her life on the hyphen between American and West Indian and was one of the first to talk of the challenges facing those who arrived from the Caribbean. She was a young mother, and perhaps for that reason, many of the gatherings were held at her apartment on Central Park West.

Like Louise, Rosa, and indeed Maya when she was in New York, the West Side was home for Paule, and her large apartment at 407 Central Park West was often the preferred venue. The high ceilings and (I guess) music-tolerant neighbors meant that we often found ourselves in her living room with the record player going. If it was chez Paule, it was party time. Then it was all about Al Green, the Motown sound, some disco favorites, and Stevie Wonder with *Talking Book* and *Innervisions*. The bass riff would come pounding off the vinyl, and Sam would start snapping his fingers and twirling and dipping to the intro beats. "Very superstitious . . ." Don't let Al Green's intro to *Love and Happiness* come on;

then it was time for some fancy footwork and special showing off. It was another night with the crowd in the era of discos and platform shoes, themed by music that transformed the world.

Rose, Louise, and Paule were stalwarts, the central folks in the group. Others came and went with less frequency but were also members in good standing of the pack. Vertamae Smart-Grosvenor, or Mae or Vert, as she was sometimes known, always provided entertainment. She had already written *Vibration Cooking*, her first book, and had been working with food as a means of cultural expression when I met her. We were both journalists at *Essence* magazine, where she penned social commentary. These pieces were witty and trenchant, and she was not afraid of taking positions that were a little controversial. "I Told Jesus It Would Be Alright If *He* Changed My Name" was an uproarious piece on the name changing to African names real or imagined that was going on in the Black community, while her book *Thursdays and Every Other Sunday Off* detailed her exploits in the world of domestic service with laughing to keep from screaming accuracy.

Baldwin declared that he loved Vertamae because she made him laugh, and indeed her exploits were the stuff of urban legend. They usually involved much to-ing and fro-ing on fire escapes and enough chases through doors to create a Feydeau farce. Her gleefully embellished retellings of them were often humorous indeed. Then there were tales of her other escapades, of her playing the vibrations as one of the Space Goddesses in the Arkestra at Sun Ra concerts (no doubt the genesis of the vibration cooking concept). Her world seemed rife with possibility; even her daughter, Kali, was a child prodigy poet with a published book, and in addition, Verta was reputed to be a grand cook.

Vertamae and I had a tenuous friendship, for like so many others in the group, she was older than I, wiser in the ways of the world than I, more volatile in personality than I, and ready to compete. With Vertamae, though, it was not about Sam. Rather, our competition began (and I'm not sure how) about my burgeoning work in the area of food and culture. I'd begun to pen a bimonthly version of my travel column in *Essence* under the rubric "The Go Gourmet" in which I wrote about the places I'd been and the foods I ate. The column was the genesis of my first cookbook, *Hot Stuff: A Cookbook in Praise of the Piquant*. Later, the culinary connections that I sampled on those journeys would form the basis for *Iron Pots and Wooden Spoons: Africa's Gifts to New World Cooking*, my second cookbook.

Verta and I both traveled in the world of the African diaspora, and we were two Black women in a field that some felt could hold only one. It was not supposed to be me. In fact, I had just stumbled into an area that allowed me to combine my love of travel, my love of food, my love of history, my love of languages, and my growing love of journalism, and it was too good a fit to let go. So we often did the diva dance, trying to figure out how to both fit together on the head of the pin that was the developing world of food studies. Over the years, we learned to appreciate each other, but for more than a little while, our bourgeoning friendship was more of a hesitation step than a waltz.

There were others, too, academics like Eleanor Traylor, with her incisive mind and enviable wardrobe, and Richard Long, who was given to larding his erudite conversation with quotes from the early philosophers in the original Greek. Some, like Stokely Carmichael, made only rare appearances; others, like Hugh Masakela, were around for a brief period and then gone; and still others—Abbey Lincoln, Max Roach, Miles Davis—appeared infrequently but made their presence immediately felt.

And then there was Nina. "Who's the bitch in the red dress?" Those words rang out across the room as I crossed the threshold. I don't remember whose home it was or what the occasion was. I do remember that I was wearing a slinky red dress made by my friend Kai Lofton that flowed liquidly over my dancer-lithe body. After looking around, I realized with a start that "the bitch in the red dress" was me. I also remember that I was staggered, but those were the first words that Nina Simone ever addressed about me. Not *to* me, *about* me! Oh my; that hadn't started well.

Naturally Sam knew Nina Simone as well. He was the one she called when an escort was a good idea and when going alone meant there was no one to fend off the crowds that might be curious. In Sam's case, his wit and intellect coupled with his dapper personal style made him a much-in-demand partner and one whose friendship the women he escorted guarded jealously. Nina was certainly in that number.

Nina had been born in North Carolina, Sam's home state, the same year and one day after Sam. Their virtual twin birth bonded them in a way that they would share and joke about. Sam had demons that she could understand, and vice versa. He had been a favorite of hers, and upon my appearance she aligned herself with the growing number of folks who felt that I was *de trop*. I was an interloper and certainly too young and naive to run with the crowd, but I had been brought by the man who was a pivot of the circle of friends and so claws were sheathed . . . somewhat.

By the mid-1970s, Simone was certainly a musical icon. I had long been a fan and often boasted that I had all of her records. Her distinctive voice and her virtuoso piano playing haunted me—"I Loves You Porgy," "Little Girl Blue," and the mordantly humorous "Four Women." Anyone with any pretense of social consciousness knew her song "Mississippi Goddamn," and many had drawn solace from "Why?

The King of Love Is Dead" following Martin Luther King Jr.'s assassination. I remember listening to it over and over again in my dorm room at college, trying to make sense of the wave of madness that had seemingly overtaken the country. Her song "To Be Young, Gifted and Black" was the anthem for my generation of young Black artists trying to figure out the world and create a place in it for themselves from which to operate with pride. It was drawn from the title of a posthumous biographical montage of the works of Lorraine Hansberry, another member of the long-standing group of friends, who had succumbed to cancer a decade before I came along. Hansberry and Simone had been friends; Nina credited Hansberry with politicizing her. Sam knew them both.

Simone's opening salvo was devastating but was mitigated somewhat when she accepted the tribute/offering that I had brought: a pair of antique Senegalese earrings that I'd purchased on a trip to that country. I remember little more of that evening other than I got through it, which is probably not a bad thing, but Nina would reappear in my life several times after that night.

Sam's international connections spread to Barbados, where Simone had traveled in 1974 and later lived. At some point, Sam had been down to visit her and met a number of folks; he returned to New York and regaled me with tales of his stay on the island. My first press trip as assistant travel editor of *Essence* also took me there, and through Sam's friendships I visited some of the places that had featured in Simone's island sojourn and met some of the folks that she'd known, including Stella St. John, wife of a former Barbadian prime minister, Bernard St. John, and her sister, Denise Hope. I saw the Island Inn hotel, where Sam had stayed, and smiled to myself remembering his commentary about the bar there and the Kingston Trio–like Merrymen who were the esteemed national musicians of Barbados of the time. That they were white and singing canned calypso-lite was uproariously amusing to us both, as it had no doubt been to the culturally attuned, highly politicized Simone. Sam described the genesis of Simone's album *It Is Finished*, and told tales of her daily practice of Rachmaninoff and Bach and other intricate pieces from the classical repertoire on her baby grand piano and how she later transformed the seemingly effortless trills and flourishes into the introductions of various songs on the album. According to him, she wanted Sam in her life in a larger way, but that was not to be; both were too volatile. On that record, Simone calls out, "Exuma, you here?" to her famous Bahamian colleague, but only I knew that Sam was also supposed to be in that audience and was not there.

My Bajan memories were not the last time that Nina intruded into my life. She would appear again, in person no less, after the heat of my relationship with Sam had transformed into cooling embers—when I was a more seasoned travel writer and journeying to Africa to report on tourism for *Travel Weekly*. I had garnered a press trip to the Ivory Coast in the days before it became the Côte d'Ivoire. By then, Simone had cemented her American exile and was living in West Africa, in Liberia, as suggested by her friend Miriam Makeba. Liberia was English speaking: the life, society, and culture were based on familiar American models, the American dollar was the official currency, and it was next door to Guinea, where Makeba lived. When Simone arrived there, the country was enjoying the last years of Americo-Liberian rule, with the descendants of former enslaved Americans living luxurious lives that would all end brutally with firing squads on a beach in the 1980 coup.

For many Liberians back then, the neighboring Ivory Coast under the presidency of Félix Houphouët-Boigny provided a spot of French sophistication and a nearby playground where perfume, champagne, haute cuisine, and haute African couture by designers like Chris Seydou and Mammadou Sy were readily available. In Abidjan, the capital, Houphouët-Boigny had created a showplace city for which he had commissioned a hotel designed to match or best anything that the West could offer. No less a critic of colonialism and its aftermath than V. S. Naipaul called it the "fairground of Abidjan." Indeed, it was.

The Hôtel Ivoire, then run by the plush Intercontinental

chain, boasted a casino, a rooftop restaurant serving Franco-Ivorian nouvelle cuisine, a lake-sized swimming pool, and an ice-skating rink. There were numerous restaurants; a massive convention center; a shopping mall featuring a bookstore, gift shop, and parfumerie; and a network of palm-fringed walks that wound their way through the property.

By this time, I had been to Abidjan several times, as both a researcher and a travel writer, stayed at the hotel more than once, and had friends who lived nearby in the Cocody area. My article was to be about the possibilities Abidjan offered for tourists, so I had revisited the markets, journeyed down to the colonial town of Grand-Bassam, and even purchased African masks and statuary at the tourist market at the downtown center of the Plateau, where the bats hung off the palm trees in clusters and swarmed nightly at sundown. I had explored the alleyways of Treichville market at length and enjoyed the mix of items from the Sahel and the Forest that came together on the vendors' tables there. I delight in markets in any form, and Treichville was particularly fascinating. There was seemingly everything, ranging from snails the size of fists in one alley to unidentifiable leafy greens in another; the small dark-skinned avocados that were so delicious with a French vinaigrette in the hotel's snack bar could be found for a pittance, and if one climbed the rickety stairs, there was a wide array of fabric, including brilliant hand-woven kente cloth from neighboring Ghana in a rainbow of colors.

One day as I was returning to my room and strolling through the hotel's shopping arcade to search for a French magazine, I was struck by a ruckus in the parfumerie that was one of the boutiques. There was shouting, and clearly the person creating the row was an American because the raised voice was in English. Hoping to defuse the situation by translating for my obviously hapless countryman, I entered and stopped short. The person bellowing was Nina Simone.

I would have backed out, but by then she'd seen me, and she remembered me! This time, I was no longer "the bitch in the red dress" but rather the individual soon to be transformed into temporary personal assistant, semi-griot, and full-time praise singer who translated her demands, got them serviced, and made sure that all knew just who she was. Following the resolution of the perfume problem, I introduced her to the more than slightly awed hotel manager, who graciously accorded her guest privileges to the hotel's swimming pool, grounds, and public rooms, which were jealously guarded perquisites of any stay and given only to Abidjan's elite who were friends of the management. He also invited her to join our scheduled dinner later in the week.

And so for two days, she became my part-time travel buddy and full-time nemesis. The next day, I invited her to join me for lunch and an afternoon at the pool. She turned up looking regal, and before settling in on the chaise at the pool, she disrobed grandly to reveal a glacial white bikini that made the most of her sleek-toned, sun-loved body and left little to the imagination. With typical Nina barbed candor, she looked at me in my swimming shroud (I've never been comfortable in bathing suits) and commented pointedly, "I'm older than you are, and my body's better than yours!" I could only nod yes in fatigued agreement, already ruing the gesture that had let foxy Nina into my personal henhouse.

Dinner with the manager at the hotel's gourmet roost, Le Toit d'Abidjan, continued the torture. She was totally charming. She'd arrived dressed to impress and pulled out all the stops worthy of the international superstar she was. She flirted, bantered lightly, and totally captivated the manager. I was so far in her shadow as to be nonexistent, which was understandable but a bit difficult because I was to interview the manager later in my stay for the newspaper. When the evening was over, I retreated to my room, closed the drapes, put the Do Not Disturb sign on the door, and took to my bed for a day, eschewing Abidjan's pleasures in order to recover.

All of Sam's friends were not always difficult for me. Others were genuine delights. Economist Mary Painter and her husband, chef Georges Garin, were very much a part of Baldwin's world; they combined Sam's and my love of France, cooking, and a good time all into one. During World War II and thereafter, the Office of Strategic Services (OSS) seems to have been an incubator for brilliant women. Painter had worked in the research and analysis section of the OSS and devised a way of using statistical models to estimate Nazi submarine capabilities with amazing accuracy.

After the war, Painter had been sent to Europe to help set up the Marshall Plan. She was a midwestern blonde who had a delicacy that camouflaged her insightful intelligence. Mary had met Baldwin in 1950 when she was working at the American embassy in Paris as an economist. She became his rock and often his salvation, and the woman he truly loved. He'd even dedicated *Another Country* to her. Richard Olney, chef, cookbook author, editor of the Time/Life Cookbook series, and good friend of both Jimmy's and Mary's, painted dual portraits of the two of them as two complementary parts of a diptych. Baldwin once said of her, "When I realized I couldn't marry Mary Painter, I realized I could marry no one." Although their intense friendship could never morph into a romantic involvement, she'd remained one of Jimmy's closest friends, seeing him through up times and down, and eventually convincing him to move to St. Paul-de-Vence in the South of France.

After a tumultuous affair, Painter had become the second wife of Georges Garin, an irascible French chef in the grand tradition. In 1961, Garin, already a renowned chef in France, sold his Hotel de la Croix Blanche in Nuits Saint Georges, Burgundy, where he'd hosted banquets for the Chevaliers du Tastevin, and left the kitchens there to open a new place in Paris near the Place Maubert. Less than a year later, the Parisian culinary upper crust had declared him one of the country's top chefs. Georges would have been spotted anywhere as a Frenchman: his bearded face was a map of the French *hexagone*, with a prominent nose just made for sniffing Cavaillon melons or fine wines.

When Mary married Georges, he'd joined her circle of friends. With her marriage, though, she'd left the world of economics and intrigue and become *la patronne* of Chez Garin, Georges's Parisian restaurant. With great pride and a nod to French restaurant tradition, she became mistress of the till or the *caissière* (the cashier and financial overseer) of her husband's spot. Nightly she would use her impressive economic skills to add up the bills at the restaurant at 9 Rue Lagrange in the fifth arrondissement on the Left Bank. She was expected to be a gracious hostess, watch over the staff, write up checks, and generally oversee the front of the house; she detested it, but kept it up for a few years.

Georges and Mary, the dual moniker by which they were known, journeyed occasionally to New York, where I met them through Sam. Georges was tickled with my French and with my developing love of food; Mary may have seen parallels between my role in Sam's life and hers in Jimmy's. Sam and I and whoever else was around would eat out together with them as Georges made his rounds of Manhattan restaurants. He was a curious eater who loved to try new things and was fascinated by the American twists on classic French food and the New York dining scene.

The restaurant scene in New York in the 1970s was breaking away from the Gallic dominance and adding a note of fun. The Forum of the Twelve Caesars used upended Roman helmets as wine buckets and referenced Roman culinary authority Acipicius in the menu listings. The Fonda del Sol was an exuberant splash of Latin American art and food that changed the palate of many New Yorkers and showcased the food of the Hispanic world in ways it would take more than twenty years to repeat. The Four Seasons, with its impeccable service, its exemplary food, and its changing seasonal decor, became a restaurant classic for all seasons, and the Brasserie brought la cuisine bourgeoise to Gotham and offered a counterpoint to the existing French restaurants that were bastions of *la grande cuisine classique*.

The city's French restaurant trend had begun with the 1964 World's Fair when the French pavilion's restaurant, helmed by the redoubtable Henri Soulé, left Flushing Meadows and became a fixture on the East Side of Manhattan known as Le Pavillon. It in turn spawned La Grenouille, La Côte Basque, La Caravelle, and others, most of them catering to well-heeled Upper East Side socialites and politicos. They became the haunts of the ladies who lunched and of Truman Capote's swans, as he called his inner circle, and were noted for presenting the most sumptuous fare in jewel box surroundings.

Georges Garin frequented these as well. He ordered with the authority of one who truly knew the food and weighed the taste of each morsel as though Paris were judging Hera, Athena, and Aphrodite. When wine was proffered for tasting, the shaking of jowls and slurping was wondrous to behold, especially as his colleagues waited, holding their breath in anticipation of his nod of approval: he was, after all, one of the best chefs in France. At La Caravelle, one of his favorites, the long, narrow entrance alley was where those who wanted to be seen roosted. Georges could care less. Wherever he sat was the best table in the house, and it usually *was* the best seat in the house. At this spot, one of the high temples of classical French cooking in New York, he was received as a demigod, and we'd file in behind him, taking our place at the table that was always heaped with delicacies.

My parents had taught me that it was polite to reciprocate, and I certainly didn't have the cash to take Georges and Mary out to a restaurant of the caliber of La Caravelle, so I invited them to my apartment for dinner. I've forgotten whether Sam was in attendance at dinner, but I think that had he been around, he might have had the kindness to restrain my youthful foolhardiness somewhat. In any case, *choucroute garnie* it was, proudly served up with much ceremony in my one-bedroom apartment with its galley kitchen and the obligatory West Village brick wall. I'd learned to love *choucroute garnie* on my first trip to Paris and have continued to love it in all its permutations from the version served at the resto U, the university canteen where I occasionally ate as a student, to those served at brasseries in Nancy, where I'd done my graduate studies. My version included sauerkraut straight from the can, frankfurters, potatoes, a can of beer, and a hearty slug of gin. It was the delight of all of my friends.

I served it straight from my yellow Le Creuset look-alike cast iron ware on my ersatz Dansk plates. It was eaten, and seconds were even requested. No commentary was made about taste, authenticity, the franks, the can of beer, the gin, or anything else. A few days later, when I next saw Georges, he brought me a small gift: a small jar of juniper berries, one of the hallmarks of the classic Alsatian *choucroute garnie*. I have no idea where he got them back then; they certainly were not grocery store staples. He said not a word of correction or of comment other than, "You might want to try these the next time that you make *choucroute*." Voilà! It was the gentlest correction I've ever received. But it resonated with me and made me like Georges and Mary even more.

I would connect with them in Paris, and, later, Sam and I would visit them with Jimmy after they moved from Paris to Soulliès-Toucas in southeastern France.

These friends—Paule, Louise, Rosa, and the rest—were folks who turned up at parties and in conversation. Though close, they were not the heart of things. That spot was reserved for Jimmy and for the special friend of Sam's who shimmered in the ether even when she was not present: Maya Angelou. Sam and Maya had been a couple, and although I had no idea of the length of time or the intensity of the romance, clearly Maya was important to Sam and he to her. I do not remember exactly when I met Maya; just one day, she was there in a whirlwind of activity.

My first remembrance of her is at a dinner at the Paparazzi, an East Side Manhattan eatery run by Jerry Purcell, the man Maya credits with being her patron and giving her enough money to keep her afloat while she was writing *I Know Why the Caged Bird Sings*. Purcell, who was a personal manager and a record, television, and concert producer, was known to those outside show business ranks as the husband of Monique van Vooren, the pneumatic Belgian actress. Through Maya, Sam knew Purcell, and we had dinner at the restaurant occasionally. Paparazzi was aptly named: it was a fishbowl restaurant with huge plate glass windows through which the diners could be seen as they tucked into their pastas.

On one occasion, Maya arrived and joined us. She was imperially tall and wore her fame like a royal mantle. By then, I had read *Caged Bird* and was already in awe of her. She breezed into the restaurant like a whirlwind, bringing more animated conversation, higher intensity, and the tension that comes with knowing that you are at the center of a vortex. It was palpable; the air had changed. Even though this was an informal gathering of friends, Maya arrived with all of the pomp of Cleopatra descending the Nile: there were kisses all around, introductions to those not known, raucous remembrances of those not in attendance, and an order of another round of drinks with which to salute the occasion.

She'd married Paul du Feu in 1973. Tall and rangy, with a finely honed sense of dry British humor, he was charming, fierce, and extremely comfortable in his masculinity. A self-proclaimed hod carrier, he was a carpenter and a bricklayer by trade and had not only been married to feminist Germaine Greer of *The Female Eunuch* fame, but had posed nude in the British *Playgirl* magazine displaying his endowments to the world. Oh yes, AND HE WAS WHITE, which in itself was sort of *scandeleux*. None of it mattered to them or to anyone else. Maya was in love; they had their own private jokes and their conspiratorial smiles. They showed up at one New York evening for dinner at Paparazzi wearing matching mink-lined denim jackets and giggling about the ridiculousness of them. Conspiratorially close, they were given to raucous behavior. Evenings might end with rousing renditions of "Knees Up Mother Brown" while dancing in lockstep down the streets or in full-throated singing of other classic pub songs. "I'm 'enry the Eighth, I am!" Paul was used to smart women, who were, as the saying went, "heavy in the head." When he was reportedly told that Maya was a very important woman in the world, his reply was, "I can carry the weight!" and for a while, he could. If he could handle Greer's notoriety, clearly he'd be able to take the weight of Maya's increasing fame.

Du Feu softened Maya in many ways and brought out her feminine side. This made her less fierce to me. Perhaps it was just that she was basking in the roseate glow of the first flush of an infatuation. Perhaps she and Sam were playing new partners off each other as former lovers occasionally do. Whatever the reason, our times with Maya and Paul had a deeper intensity, as though all other things had suddenly been squared. This, I would learn, was the way of their world: profound conversations about all aspects of life, heart-felt rage tempered by equally intense laughter with heads thrown back and their entire bodies poured into the moment. It was a time of life lived fully, deeply. Random encounters would smoothly morph into dinners or gatherings that would then be transformed into events that could go well into the wee hours of the morning, but always underneath it all, there was the heartbeat of work and writing and speaking and teaching and all of the daily madness of life.

Sam thrived on it all, and I learned like a wise moth not to fly too close to the flames, but to hover in the middle distance, close enough to be a part of the circle and yet not so close that I was likely to get burned when the intensity of the conversations or the depth of the emotion turned caustic and corrosive. And so it went. As I became more a part of the group, however tangential, I was grudgingly welcomed and then accepted as a sort of appendage of Sam. It was fine, because it allowed me to sit in the room or hang out with them wherever he went—uptown, downtown, or around the world.

Choucroute Garnie à Ma Manière

I love the Alsatian sauerkraut dish known as choucroute garnie *that I sampled on my first trip to the City of Light. Somehow it just means Paris to me. I will always cringe at the thought of my early version of this classic. Now I'm a bit more sophisticated and yes, I make a point of using juniper berries.*

– Serves ten to twelve –

1¾ pounds smoked meaty ham hocks

8 ounces thick-sliced bacon strips, cut into 1-inch pieces

2 large onions, chopped

1 teaspoon juniper berries (you may substitute ½ cup gin)

1 teaspoon whole black peppercorns

10 whole cloves

8 whole allspice berries

3 bay leaves

2 (2-pound) jars sauerkraut, rinsed and then squeezed dry

2½ cups dry white wine

2 pounds kielbasa and knockwurst, cut into 4-inch pieces

1 pound frankfurters with natural casings

1½ pounds small Yukon Gold potatoes

Place the ham hocks in large saucepan. Add enough water to well cover the hocks. Bring to a boil. Reduce the heat, cover, and simmer until the meat is very tender, about 2 hours. Transfer the hocks to a medium bowl. Reserve 2½ cups of the broth. Remove the meat from the bones. Discard the bones and place the meat back in the bowl.

Preheat the oven to 350°F. Heat a large, heavy pot over medium-high heat. Add the bacon and sauté until it is crisp. Using a slotted spoon, place the bacon in the bowl with the meat.

Add the onions, juniper berries, peppercorns, cloves, allspice, and bay leaves to the same pot in which you cooked the bacon. Sauté until the onions are tender, about 5 minutes. Mix in the sauerkraut. Add the reserved broth, the wine, and the gin, if using. Add all the meats and press to submerge them. Boil for 10 minutes, then cover the *choucroute*, place in the oven, and bake for 1½ hours.

Meanwhile, cook the potatoes separately in a pot of boiling salted water until tender. Remove the bay leaves and arrange the sauerkraut, meats, and potatoes on one large, deep platter. Serve with a variety of mustards.

Chapter Five

OH, THE PLACES YOU'LL GO!
WEST SIDE RAMBLES

The folks my age who still lived in Queens were either starting families or still attached to parental apron strings. In
Manhattan, there was a serious disdain for the "bridge and
tunnel" folks. We were identifiable by our tendency to refer
to Manhattan as "The City" as though it glowed emerald
on the horizon beyond our boroughs, which were in fact
equally a part of "the city" in question. As a newly emanci-
pated member of the B&T crowd, I did my best to evidence
what I thought was Manhattan sophistication. My crew of
friends—others who had escaped the outer boroughs like
me, those from out of town, and those who had grown up in
Harlem—socialized in our newly acquired apartments. We
haunted local restaurants, savored the independence of our
twenties, and reveled in our veneer of worldliness.

In the early 1970s, some of my friends from the High

School of Performing Arts had garnered jobs at the nascent PBS, working on a show with Ellis Haizlip called *Soul*. The jobs allowed them the flexibility to pursue auditions and nurture their burgeoning acting careers. Working on the show also allowed them to make contact with anyone who was anyone in the world of the Black Arts. Haizlip's show was brilliant; it was don't-miss-television for every Black intellectual in the city. The guests ranged from political activists like Stokely Carmichael and the mother of George Jackson, one of the in-the-news Soledad Brothers, to poets like Victor Hernández Cruz, Jayne Cortez, and Felipe Luciano of the Last Poets, an early spoken-word group. Imani, a young African American poet, was an occasional guest, and his love poem "The Water of Your Bath" remained framed and hanging in my bathroom over the tub for more than forty years.

Music was an important component of the show, which introduced wider audiences to jazz musicians like pianist Herbie Hancock, bassist Ron Carter, and Rahsaan Roland Kirk. Authors were not left out. Chester Himes, author of *Cotton Comes to Harlem*, Amiri Baraka, Louise Meriwether, and Vertamae Smart-Grosvenor all appeared, and there was a notable two-part show hosted by Nikki Giovanni with a single guest: Baldwin himself. Then there were the popular singers. Here again Haizlip excelled, and many performers debuted on *Soul* while others made the show their television home. Esther Phillips, Bill Withers, Miriam Makeba, and Gladys Knight and the Pips all graced the stage, as did Nick Ashford and Valerie Simpson before their first album was released. On occasions when *Soul* produced musical stars in cabaret performances and needed an audience, they'd invite me and other friends, and I'd doll up, head out, sit at one of the small nightclub tables that decorated the set, and listen to the greats perform live for free. I still can recall the frisson of being in the second row of a notable performance with Al Green distributing blood-red roses to the women in the small audience while crooning "Let's, Let's Stay Together." The show ended before I became a part of the Baldwin crowd through my friendship with Sam, but *Soul* and its stars and hosts defined and influenced Black intellectual life of the 1970s throughout the country at a time when the cultural presence of African Americans and the civil rights movement and its ongoing struggle made us a focus of the world. I knew many of the players in Baldwin's crowd from my time at *Soul* where I would hang out in the office with friends and bask in their proximity to fame. We had even formed a loose club called Roots, designed to spread the gospel of Black Arts. The club was the genesis of my writing career and the source of some lifelong friends like photographer John Pinderhughes.

• • •

Many of my friends lived on the increasingly popular Upper West Side where the rents were cheaper than in the Village and the apartments much larger. My job in Queens, though, tethered me to the IND/Independent subway line and I was happily nestled in the West Village near the E and F trains. The taxi or subway ride uptown on the IRT became a regular weekend commute as we zipped back and forth for gatherings.

We all led peripatetic lives within Manhattan. New York has always been a city of neighborhoods that are as distinct as villages, each with its own ethos and special spots. Sam had adopted some of Baldwin's poles as his own, and so we journeyed uptown where Baldwin had grown up and where his mother, known as "Mother Baldwin," lived. There was the West Village where we lived, anchored by Sam's Horatio Street apartment and mine on Jane Street, and a jazz club on the West Side of Manhattan.

Mother Baldwin's home was special and seen only by the intimate inner circle. There, Jimmy was comfortable in the heart of his family. Fame often distances "golden ones" from friends and family. That was not the case with Baldwin; he was blessed. His family remained a family, and he was treated as another member, albeit a famous one, within the circle. His siblings, Wilmer (known to all as Lover), Paula, Gloria, Barbara, and David, encircled him with their families and friends. Jimmy in turn brought his closest into the fold and on occasions when the nights became long, we all sometimes repaired to Mother Baldwin's and the rooms rang with laughter and family conversation. Frank Karefa-Smart, Gloria's husband then, told tall tales of his life in his native Sierra Leone, and Helen Brodie Baldwin, Lover's wife, sang bawdy camp songs from her days at Camp Minisink. (This iconic camp for Black New Yorkers was in Dutchess County and was founded by the New York Mission Society; it was the first sleep-away camp for many African American children.) At these times, life affirmed the ordinary everyday existence of Baldwin's nuclear family. Of course, we occasionally witnessed the squabbles of siblings, but we were also there for the celebrations of the stops along life's journey: birthdays, weddings, anniversaries, and more.

In Greenwich Village in Baldwin's former apartment building at 81 Horatio Street, Sam's apartment was also special and reserved for intimates who passed muster and could hold their own with his rapier-sharp tongue. The crowd was larger than the one that gathered at Mother Baldwin's, and the level of discourse was often more academic in tenor, with conversation time given to English instruction, the Black Arts Movement, and comparisons of the level of education at Historically Black Colleges and Universities (HBCUs) as opposed to that at traditionally white schools. (Sam, a graduate of North Carolina College, was a fervent partisan for and supporter of HBCUs.) Other of Sam's friends, like

Richard Long of Atlanta University and Eleanor Traylor of Howard University, were also products of these mainly southern schools and agreed on their rigorous education and their merit. I was a recent graduate of decidedly white Bryn Mawr, where my class, with the largest number of Blacks to that date, had numbered six of us. So I simply listened to their debates, thinking of the dedicated folks I met at the all-Black College Language Association meetings that Sam insisted I attend, and learned to love and began to understand and value many of the empowering elements of what was then a classic HBCU education.

When the event had been planned in advance, Sam's table groaned with homemade pâtés, roasts, southern-style vegetables, and more. At other times, El Faro was called, someone was dispatched down the street, and we dined on shrimp in green sauce and fruit-flavored barbecued spare ribs. El Faro was the public face of this Village location, but the private one was within the confines of Sam's small place.

The third locus of Baldwin's New York was the most public venue: Mikell's, a jazz club named for its owner, Mike Mikell. Today's prosperous Upper West Side of fancy boutiques and exotic restaurants is home to a white liberal intelligentsia, but this was not yet the West Side norm in the early 1970s. It was a neighborhood on the rise, but the terrain was a good deal more rugged. For those who veered off the beaten path, it, like the West Village, could be dangerous. New York is an organic city, one that is always in transition. Within a lifetime (often in only a few decades) neighborhoods grow, gain prominence, peak, and return to oblivion.

Blacks had traditionally lived in San Juan Hill, the area south of Sixty-seventh Street, since the turn of the twentieth century. It was demolished in the late 1950s to make way for the construction of Lincoln Center. The hood's last gasp was even recorded on film as the former old-line tenements with their cramped rooms and their fire escapes did their last public duty before demolition as the sets for the movie *West Side Story*. Those displaced from the buildings where Maria and Tony, Bernardo and Anita danced their way to an Oscar for best picture moved northward into the burgeoning area that would become today's West Side.

Riverside Drive had always been ritzy, although you might not want to cross into the park. West End Avenue's high-ceilinged, multiroomed apartments also attracted the wealthy, as did buildings on Central Park West, with their stunning park views. The midsection of the neighborhood, with Columbus as the commercial strip and Amsterdam housing smaller shops and low-rent apartments, offered the displaced a place to be. Southern Blacks, Dominicans, Puerto Ricans, Cubans, and Eastern European Jews made the area home from the 1940s through the 1960s, establishing themselves in the grand apartment buildings that existed among much-reduced surroundings. By the *Mad Men* era of the late 1960s and early 1970s, the area was still the Wild, Wild West. But townhouses were being renovated and apartments slowly being turned into co-ops or condos. The apartments were grand, and the brownstones were bastions of nineteenth-century glory. However, around many corners, drug addicts, welfare hotels, and appalling schools still lurked. Changes, though, were happening rapidly, and gentrification was on the way. On June 30, 1969, *New York* magazine reported:

> That huge, sprawling, alternate-side-of-the-street society filled with shabby low-rent housing and Oscar Lewis runaways is changing fast. "In five years," one city planner said, "the only dumpy little shopping bag ladies you'll be able to find on the West Side will be stuffed and behind glass at the Museum of Natural History."

In the year of that statement, Mike Mikell and his wife, Pat, opened a jazz joint on the corner of Ninety-seventh Street and Columbus Avenue. It was around the corner from Park West Village, a government-subsidized urban redevelopment project designed to provide affordable rentals with "fresh air, good light, and attractive landscaped grounds for middle income people." Greenwich Village had provided green spaces and apartments with reasonable rents that had attracted an earlier generation of writers, artists, dancers, actors, and others who toiled at the impecunious end of fame's equation. By the 1960s, they were being priced out of the increasingly gentrifying Village, and those who were not quite bohemian enough to relish the true grit of the developing East Village and Alphabet City headed to the Upper West Side, lured by the reasonable rents and the huge apartments, many of which boasted all of the amenities of a bygone era such as maids' rooms, service entrances, back stairways, and in-house storage.

The West Side was home for Maya Angelou, Rosa Guy, Louise Meriwether, and Paule Marshall. Guy found an apartment in the newly constructed Park West Village and established a beachhead. When Maya moved to New York, she roomed with Rosa until she got her own place, also in Park West Village. When Louise Meriwether arrived from California, she joined them in the complex that had become a West Side mecca for many of the Black intelligentsia. Amid the townhouses and gentrifying tenements of the West Side, Park West Village's spread-out, low buildings with grassy common spaces stood out and became part of a West Side hub that attracted many other African American artists and writers to the neighborhood. Bassist Ron Carter and singer Harry Belafonte lived in the same building on West End

Avenue. Actor Morgan Freeman, before he became a mega-star, was another neighborhood denizen, and *Essence*'s editor in chief, Marcia Ann Gillespie, bought a place next door to the Dakota. Susan Taylor, editor in chief to be, roosted near Lincoln Center. Gentrification had begun.

A critical mass of working Black folk with disposable income changed the neighborhood's social life and resulted in the opening of several restaurants created by and for the new clientele. The Only Child Restaurant on the downtown perimeter of the neighborhood at 226 West Seventy-ninth Street offered not only food but poetry readings by a grow-ing roster of African American writers who were part of the thriving Black Arts Movement. A listing in *Black World/ Negro Digest* for August 1974 informs that previous artists to ascend the podium included writers Tom Weatherly Jr., Lynn Shorter, Mervyn Taylor, Judy Simmons, and Elouise Loftin.

The Cellar at Ninety-fifth and Columbus, run by leg-endary Black restaurateur Howard Johnson, was more in the center of the West Side zone. The restaurant catered to the developing new Black intelligentsia and business folk who were part of the neighborhood's gentrification. It was a meeting point and a focal point and even boasted an inter-racial, although predominantly Black, crowd. These new restaurants were not soul food joints but relatively expensive white-tablecloth neighborhood venues where menu items included chef salads, shrimp scampi, and, as a touch of Europe, French onion soup.

Under the Stairs on Columbus between Ninety-third and Ninety-fourth completed the dining triumvirate. It was a neighborhood spot, but for most people, it passed for sophisticated and at any hour of the evening was a hive of energy and activity. The Columbus Avenue strip (albeit only four short blocks) was a veritable Bermuda Triangle of social activity into which more than one unsuspecting young woman got lost running between the three places looking for friends and never quite finding them but usually finding a grand time no matter what.

Mikell's, located at the center of this pulsing Upper West Side zone, completed the list of nearby venues and was the third pole in Baldwin's NYC life. It offered jazz and good stiff drinks, along with some prime people-watching, and had become *the* place on the music scene and the spot where the evening was guaranteed to end up whether it began in one of the neighborhood places or even down in the Village. Mikell's was a hub of Black social activity on the West Side and all around the town. On any given evening, folks from nearby Park West Village could be found propping up the bar, along with school principals and medical professionals. There was usually a goodly smattering of beautiful young women in a range of hues. Many were just emerging fried, dried, and blown to the side from El Yunque (later El Yunque Oba), the city's preeminent Black beauty salon, helmed by Ruth Sanchez and often promoted by *Essence* magazine—required reading material for any Black woman who wanted to be in the know. The women crossed Mikell's threshold in search of a partner for life or a warm shoulder for the evening in times before booty calls but after the opening gong of women's sexual liberation that was sounded by the Pill. El Yunque's proximity, complete with the models, would-be models, wannabe models, and freshly "done" well-groomed young single women it disgorged into the neighborhood probably explained the number of single—or not-so-single—men who were regulars at the bar.

Stand-out faces in the crowd included surgeon Leo Maitland, "doctor to the stars," who had treated Miles Davis and Geoffrey Holder, who was a regular, as was school principal, activist, and parents' rights advocate Ron Evans, who had been at the center of the Ocean Hill–Brownsville school conflict between the common school board and the New York City teachers' union. Timothy Fales, husband of Josephine Premise, father of socialite and culture vulture Susan Fales-Hill, and scion of the Philadelphia family that gave their name and some of their money to NYU, was also often in attendance at the end of the bar, where patrons were usually three deep and people jockeyed for elbow room and prayed for a seat.

Jazz was the background music, and the club hosted most of the major stars of the period. Stuff, the house band that was formed in 1974, played three times a week. It was considered one of the best bands in the city and created a sound all its own, combining soul, funk, and jazz. The atmosphere was welcoming, the drinks kept flowing, and rumor had it that other substances were available downstairs. The house musicians were so polished and professional that major stars loved to sit in with them. Stevie Wonder might show up one night and Joe Cocker another to polish his "soul chops" with folks who really knew. Whitney Houston made her solo debut there one evening when her mother, Cissy Houston, who was scheduled to sing, tricked her daughter into performing by claiming to be too ill to go on. Later, Whitney would be heard by record mogul Clive Davis of Arista Records during another Mikell's engagement and offered a contract. Many of the musicians who had appeared as guests on *Soul* left those studios and headed over to Mikell's to end the evening jamming with friends. Later, after *Soul* was canceled in 1972, they would use Mikell's as a hangout. Paul Shaffer, leader of David Letterman's late house band, declared Mikell's "soul heaven," and indeed for many it was.

It wasn't all about music, though. Mikell's was a literary as well as a musical landmark. Journalists and those whom they were covering, as well as literary lights, all met up at Mikell's, including Charlayne Hunter-Gault, Novella Nelson, Vertamae Smart-Grosvenor, and Jayne Cortez. Jimmy and his world also made this spot their spot. In so doing, they made it a cultural epicenter of Black New York life. Writer Louise Meriwether said simply about Mikell's, "We felt safe there." Indeed, it was a haven for all.

Presiding behind the bar, juggling its disparate personalities with the dexterity of a master magician, was Jimmy's baby brother, David Baldwin. Although Jimmy was David's half-brother, they, and indeed all of the Baldwin family members, shared a resemblance that was undeniable. (Clearly Mother Baldwin had some strong genes.) With David, it was all in the forehead, the eyes, and the teeth. He was taller and handsomer than Jimmy in a more conventional way. Like his more famous sibling, he was blessed with the gift of gab and an ability to speak with all, which was an undeniable asset to his work as a bartender. He also had some of the quicksilver energy of his older sibling. Yet in each of them, there was something else: a twinkle in their eyes that was backed with an ineffable sadness. Like Jimmy, David had a wicked sense of humor and a kindness that was overarching. He also shared Jimmy's ability to dance in many different circles and knew how to keep a party going. In their youth, Jimmy, as the older brother, had tried to shield younger David from some of life's vicissitudes and to smooth the path that he knew awaited him as a Black man, so they were close. If there was any one individual in the world for whom Jimmy would walk to hell and back, it was David. At Mikell's, behind the bar, though, David Baldwin was a star in his own firmament.

In the 1970s, Mikell's was the special hub of that world, where to cross the threshold was to know that something important was going on, something new was being created. Even though it heaved with activity and was a truly happening bar, something else was at work at Mikell's. The place had a sense of possibility that was palpable. It was a spot where the world was debated and re-created nightly. If Mikell's was the super circus of the West Side, David was its ringmaster.

For many, the world of the West Side consisted of Mikell's, the Bermuda triangle of restaurants, and their apartments or those of their friends. For Sam, though, those spots were only one part of his Upper West Side equation. For him, the West Side also meant Lincoln Center and especially the opera. Whether because of the European culture that it represented or through a real affinity for the music (although this was tantamount to heresy in the Black Power 1970s), Sam was a true lover of opera. He was multifaceted in ways that defied description, and I knew he was cantankerous enough to refuse to be put into any one type of cultural box.

Christmas, a holiday he despised, was given over to a day of serious scotch drinking, accompanied by maudlin musings pronounced over a soundtrack of Bessie Smith and Ma Rainey. But he was equally driven to hear soprano Jessye Norman's debut concert at Alice Tully Hall in 1973, where he hummed along with the Schubert *leider* and commented knowledgably on the interpretation.

As one whose culture-vulture parents had subscriptions to all of the theaters at the opening of Lincoln Center and who had cut her Metropolitan Opera teeth in the score desk seats in the Old Met, I was a willing partner in his adventures in the world of classical music. My mother volunteered for the Metropolitan Opera Association and was often given house seats for the performances, so we benefited from those as well. In those days, everything was beautiful at the opera. Folks still dressed up, and the lights were shiny and new and ascended to the ceiling, announcing one's entry into a world of magic and music. My 1974 date book lists my opera-going selections: *Tales of Hoffmann* by Sutherland, *I Puritani* with Beverly Sills, *Les Troyens* with Shirley Verrett and Christa Ludwig, and *Manon Lescaut* with Leontyne Price. There were others as well—some twenty-one in all—and so it was a round of opera performances spent listening to the voices of the midcentury: Sutherland, Horne, Pavarotti, Te Kanawa, Milnes, Domingo, and von Stade. There were notable conductors and even James Levine's Met debut.

There were as well the Black divas who were staking a claim and ascending to the operatic stratosphere: Bumbry, Grist, Battle, and the grand divas—Leontyne Price and Martina Arroyo, both of whom Sam knew.

There, as everywhere else he went in the world, Sam was a friend of the famous. So we went backstage after a performance by Leontyne Price to see her in her dressing room, and I will always remember her kind words to me, "Who is this pretty lady?" I smiled, tongue-tied and floating on air at meeting the *diva assoluta*. Sam chatted companionably, while I drank it all in: the floral tributes, the champagne, and myriad reflections of the votaries that we were in the dressing room mirrors; the wig stands and costumes, and even the discarded makeup towels soiled with brown greasepaint; the palpable air of glamour and international success counterpointed by the backstage realities of performance delighted me. It was heady air indeed for a former High School of Performing Arts student who had once harbored dreams of performance.

Then there was Martina Arroyo, the diva from Harlem who'd gone to Hunter High School. She was a closer friend of Sam's, so there were not only backstage visits but on more than one occasion dinner at her apartment in the company of other opera stars and her mother, who took great delight in deflating Sam and taking my part. The musical divas were kinder to me than the literary ones, perhaps because their emotional attachment to Sam was not as great. In any case, they were balm to my soul that was becoming wounded from flying too close to the stars and breathing air that was too rarefied.

Hanging out with Sam was not all opera and champagne. There were difficulties and hurts and slights from Sam's quicksilver personality, which could go from warm to icy in the beat of a hummingbird's wing. I vividly recall being all dressed up to attend Jessye Norman's Met debut in dual roles of Dido and Cassandra in *Les Troyens*. My mother had been given tickets. I have no idea why they were available for such a performance, but they were, and for box seats no less, albeit on the side: I was becoming a picky connoisseur. I waited on the plaza for Sam to appear, late and breathless as usual. The bells rang, the doors were closing, and so I scurried up the grand staircase solo, fully expecting that he would arrive later and be stuck in the waiting room until the first interval. I fidgeted through the first act wondering what had happened and if he had made it in under the wire in the era before cell phones made everything checkable. When he hadn't appeared by the second act, I was anxious and disappointed, and hurt and angry (although I dared not even admit it to myself). Finally I realized that I was too distracted and on the verge of tears to enjoy the excitement of the moment. I was in such a state by the second interval that I picked up my program, headed out into the night, hailed a taxi, and went home to lick my wounds in private. When Sam surfaced later that evening after multiple worried telephone calls, he was fine and pugnaciously dared me to say anything other than, "What happened?" That question was met with a temper flair and a cavalier, "I got busy," with no apology in sight. That, though, was in the waning years of our relationship. When times were good, they were very, very good, but it had been going on like that for more than a decade. I was tired of, but kind of used to, Sam's mercurial ways, so it got buried with the other slights and wounds and never again mentioned.

In the good times when Sam showed up and his temper was in check, there was music, possibly a backstage visit, and then usually a post-opera dinner across the avenue at Le Poulailler, Robert Meyzen's (of midtown's La Caravelle) West Side venue that was the Sardi's of the opera world. No less a culinary light than Craig Claiborne had written about the spot: "In the beginning Henri Soulé begat Le Pavillon and La Côte Basque. Le Pavillon begat La Caravelle and Le Poulailler."

These restaurants served as the genesis of many, not to say all, of the grand French restaurants in New York in the final third of the twentieth century, so the food at Le Poulailler was splendid and the service impeccable. *New York* magazine's restaurant critic, Gael Greene, declared it "the comeliest restaurant within sprinting distance of Zubin's imperious baton." It also appealed to Sam and my mutual love of France. The menu offered classic French fare with some lighter dishes on the post-theater menu, and I was especially fond of the *gougonettes de sole*, divine fish fingers that made for perfect late-night eating as we waited on the red leather banquettes for the singers to enter amid bravos from the diners.

While Le Poulailler was our preferred spot, there were other places as well. In later years, entrepreneur Howard Sanders, coproducer of Josephine Baker's last New York show and Eartha Kitt's triumphant 1974 return from self-imposed exile, and another friend of Sam's, became part owner of a short-lived restaurant and cabaret at 1 Lincoln Plaza on Broadway across from Lincoln Center named Cleo's. It offered a full menu, flower vendors who floated among the diners offering their wares, the occasional strolling fortune-teller, and a roster of jazz performers who were known to aficionados. Cleo's also boasted headliners and was anchored by occasional appearances by the great Mabel Mercer, who left the St. Regis room that had been named for her to sing there. It quickly became our alternate post-opera venue and often a destination in itself.

Cleo's differed from Le Poulailler in that it appealed not only to opera aficionados and music lovers but also a unique mix of people: heiresses of dubious provenance, no-count counts, and I'm sure more than a few con men and hustlers roamed the floor alongside the West Side Black bourgeoisie and the neighborhood curious in a twentieth-century potpourri of folks who could have been transplanted from Bricktop's Paris Club in the 1920s, where Mercer had also sung. A small advertisement in the back pages of the October 4, 1976, issue of *New York* magazine proclaims, "Lady with a Voice. Mabel Mercer in one of her all-too-rare singing appearances opens October 5th at Cleo's."

Sam and I were probably in the audience. Sam had introduced me to Mabel Mercer while she was still singing at the St. Regis. Mercer's trajectory was extraordinary. Her career had enough twists and turns to make several miniseries: she had understudied the great African American performer Florence Mills and performed in minstrel show troupes. Mercer had sung Cole Porter songs to Cole Porter, danced with the prince of Wales (Edward, that is), and entertained celebrities like Ernest Hemingway, Coco Chanel, Colette, and the Maharani of Cooch Behar: the upper crust of the period.

By the time that I met her with Sam, she was a legend, and her renditions of songs were the *générique* theme songs of our relationship. We'd head up to the St. Regis or to Cleo's and station ourselves at a ringside table and listen to her sing in a quavering voice that had become less crystalline with age but no less poignant and still able to evoke all manner of emotion. When she sang "Why Did I Choose You?" I mused on that question myself looking over at Sam with romance in my eyes and at the same time wondering why he had in fact chosen me.

Our nights listening to Mabel were magical. Mercer and her music inspired Sam. He'd even written about her in one of the rare articles that he would pull out of the coffee table drawer where he kept all of his writings and read to his enraptured public after the liquor had flowed at a dinner party or a Sunday gathering. It began with a description of Mercer from which I recall only the mention of her dress as being made from "funeral parlor drapes." Indeed, Mercer was given to heavy brocades that artfully clothed her ample figure. By the time that I met her, she would sit in a straight-backed chair with the impeccable posture that she'd probably been imprinted with at her convent boarding school in England, cross her hands in her lap, and sing. Oh Lord, could she sing, in tones that would create a world in front of our eyes. I was transfixed not only by the songs but the understanding of many of the lyrics for the first time. From British songs like "Chase Me Charlie" by Noel Coward to classics like "Down in the Depths on the Ninetieth Floor" to contemporary songs like "It's Not Easy Being Green," the Kermit the Frog song from *Sesame Street*, she led me to listen to lyrics in a different way. I could certainly see how Sinatra and other great twentieth-century performers claimed that she had taught them about phrasing.

By then, I was not at all surprised that Sam knew her well (he seemed to know everyone), and she would on occasion come and sit with us between sets. We would exchange casual conversation and compare notes about our cats: Sam's Blues, my Askia and Mouss, and hers. She had a series of them and delighted in telling us when they were away—"at camp," as she referred to the boarding facility where they were occasionally kept when she was away from home.

The haute culture of Le Poulailler and the European sophistication of Cleo's were the counterpoint to the sho' nuff reality of Mikell's and its activity. In a real way, they exemplified the complexity of Sam's nature, with one side vying with the other for primacy. Each completed him, with the opera providing another West Side hub: one linked to a different world from his in the Village or the one at Queens SEEK, but one in which Sam was no less comfortable. In our years together, I learned to traverse those worlds and to function in each of them with the range of folks whom Sam knew.

Goujonnettes de Sole with Ersatz Sauce Gribiche

An after-opera dinner at Le Poulailler was always a joyous meal. But it was usually around midnight, so light fare was called for. These bites of sole were perfect: fish sticks for the gods. They satisfied the need for food and yet weren't so heavy that they prevented sleep. At Le Poulailler, they were served with a sauce gribiche, a creamy mayonnaise-like sauce prepared from hard-boiled egg yolks, oil, and vinegar with mustard, chervil, tarragon, capers, and chopped gherkins. I cheat and add the ingredients to a very good store-bought mayonnaise.

– Serves four –

6 flounder or sole fillets, about
   1¼ pounds
1 medium egg
Salt and freshly ground pepper
   to taste

¼ cup flour
3 cups bread crumbs
4 cups canola oil, or enough for
   deep-frying
1 lemon, cut into thin slices

There is an indentation down the center of each fillet. Place the fillets on a flat surface and cut down the center, making two parallel slices on either side of the bone line. Remove and discard the bone line. Cut each fillet half on the diagonal into ½-inch-thick strips.

Combine the egg, salt, pepper, and 2 tablespoons of water in a small bowl and beat well with a whisk. Pour the mixture into a flat dish for dipping.

Place the flour on one plate and the bread crumbs on another.

Season the fish strips with salt and pepper and dredge first in the flour. (Each piece should be coated with flour, but shake to remove excess.)

Then dip the fish strips in the egg mixture and coat with the bread crumbs. Press lightly with a knife to make the bread crumbs adhere. Roll on a flat surface using one palm.

Heat the oil in a skillet or wok to 375°F and add the fish strips, about twelve at a time. Turn gently as they cook. Do not overcrowd the pieces in the oil or they will not brown evenly. Cooking time is about 2 minutes per batch.

Continue cooking until all the pieces are done. Drain on paper towels and serve with the lemon slices and the sauce.

Ersatz Sauce Gribiche

Makes about 1½ cups

1 cup very good mayonnaise
1 teaspoon Dijon mustard
1 teaspoon minced chervil
1 teaspoon minced tarragon

1 teaspoon chopped capers
3 French small cornichon pickles, minced

Combine all the ingredients in a small bowl, stirring to make sure the herbs, capers, and pickles are evenly distributed throughout. Serve room temperature along with the *goujonnettes*.

Goujonnettes de Sole with Ersatz Sauce Gribiche

An after-opera dinner at Le Poulailler was always a joyous meal. But it was usually around midnight, so light fare was called for. These bites of sole were perfect: fish sticks for the gods. They satisfied the need for food and yet weren't so heavy that they prevented sleep. At Le Poulailler, they were served with a sauce gribiche, *a creamy mayonnaise-like sauce prepared from hard-boiled egg yolks, oil, and vinegar with mustard, chervil, tarragon, capers, and chopped gherkins. I cheat and add the ingredients to a very good store-bought mayonnaise.*

– Serves four –

6 flounder or sole fillets, about 1¼ pounds	¼ cup flour
1 medium egg	3 cups bread crumbs
Salt and freshly ground pepper to taste	4 cups canola oil, or enough for deep-frying
	1 lemon, cut into thin slices

There is an indentation down the center of each fillet. Place the fillets on a flat surface and cut down the center, making two parallel slices on either side of the bone line. Remove and discard the bone line. Cut each fillet half on the diagonal into ½-inch-thick strips.

Combine the egg, salt, pepper, and 2 tablespoons of water in a small bowl and beat well with a whisk. Pour the mixture into a flat dish for dipping.

Place the flour on one plate and the bread crumbs on another.

Season the fish strips with salt and pepper and dredge first in the flour. (Each piece should be coated with flour, but shake to remove excess.)

Then dip the fish strips in the egg mixture and coat with the bread crumbs. Press lightly with a knife to make the bread crumbs adhere. Roll on a flat surface using one palm.

Heat the oil in a skillet or wok to 375°F and ad[ ] about twelve at a time. Turn gently as they cook. Do n[ ] pieces in the oil or they will not brown evenly. Cook[ ] 2 minutes per batch.

Continue cooking until all the pieces are done. Dr[ ] els and serve with the lemon slices and the sauce.

Ersatz Sauce Gribiche

Makes about 1½ cups

1 cup very good mayonnaise	1 teaspoon chopp[ ]
1 teaspoon Dijon mustard	3 French small co[ ]
1 teaspoon minced chervil	minced
1 teaspoon minced tarragon	

Combine all the ingredients in a small bowl, stirrin[ ] herbs, capers, and pickles are evenly distributed[ ] room temperature along with the *goujonnettes.*

Caldo Gallego—Galician White Bean Soup

I first tasted caldo gallego on a trip to Santiago de Compostela more years ago than I want to count. It was love at first slurp: the combination of the slightly spicy chorizo sausage, the bland starch of the potato, and the tang of the greens was perfectly suited to that northern Spanish town where they boast they have made rainfall an art form. I was thrilled to discover it on the menu at El Faro, where many chowed down on shrimp in green sauce and other shellfishy delights. It rapidly became my go-to order: comfort in a bowl. Even today, one spoonful takes me time-traveling back to the scarred wooden booths in the restaurant's back room and reminds me of my youth.

– Serves six –

1 ham hock (about ½ pound)
2 tablespoons olive oil
1 medium yellow onion, cut into ¼-inch-thick slices
¼ pound chorizo, cut into ¼-inch-thick rounds
¾ pound Yukon Gold potatoes (about 2 medium), peeled and cut into ¾-inch-thick cubes

2 cups small white turnips, roughly chopped
2 cans cannellini beans and their liquid
4 cups chopped kale
Salt and freshly ground black pepper

Prepare the ham hock by cooking it in water to cover for 2 hours. Reserve the cooking liquid and add enough water to make 10 cups.

In a large, heavy saucepot over medium-high heat, heat the oil. Add the onions and chorizo and cook until the onions soften and the chorizo starts to brown, about five minutes.

Add the ham hock and liquid, the potatoes, and the turnips. Reduce the heat to medium-low. Simmer, stirring occasionally, skimming off and discarding any foam that rises to the surface, until the ham, potatoes, and turnips soften, about 1½ hours.

Add the beans and the kale and cook until the greens are tender, about 20 minutes.

Remove the ham hock. Pull the meat off the bone and discard the bone. Stir the meat into the pot. Adjust seasonings and serve.

Chapter Six

WANDERLUST:
SONOMA, HAITI, AND PARIS

Travel has always been a part of my life, whether I was dreaming about it in my early years or writing about it and doing it in my later ones. It was only natural that Sam and I would travel together to visit some of his friends or in my capacity as a travel editor. We traveled well together. I was the organizer, accompanying foil, and, when funds got slim, occasional wallet; Sam presented me to his friends, and I got to enjoy having a plus one when permitted on a press trip. Our first joint excursion was an important one, as it cemented our couplehood. We went to visit Maya and Paul in Sonoma.

Sonoma is a different place today, touting itself on the Web as a short ride from San Francisco and adjacent to the better-known Napa. It's always been sort of Napa's less-favored younger sister. California was unknown territory to me. I vaguely knew some of the French wine regions: I'd visited Champagne and sampled bubbly in the limestone caves there and sipped my way along the *route de vin* in Alsace—Ribeauvillé, Riquewihir, Haut-Koenigsbourg, and more—but the California informality of the wine country and the joie de vivre and European style of living took me by surprise. It was a very different part of the world from the Upper West Side and Greenwich Village, where I usually saw Maya. When we visited, it was a time of cooking and visiting Maya's friends, telling tales, and observing Maya in her natural habitat. Sam had been invited to spend a week and he asked me to join him, perhaps as a shield against feeling left out of Maya's newfound domestic bliss.

Maya had a home in a Mediterranean-looking town of red-tile roofs complete with a guesthouse in which we were comfortably ensconced. At dinnertime we went up to the main house. The kitchen had an open plan, and there was a large island in the middle. There was also a fireplace in the dining area and Maya burned lavender in a fire shovel, which perfumed the entire space with a wonderful aroma. It was a lovely trick and would take the pungency of the curry that she was going to cook out of the air. Then it was time to cook; the meal was an eight-boy curry. Maya explained that the "boys" were named for the number of servants who would carry the condiments to the table. And there could be as many as twelve or fifteen. The dish was not a curry in the classic Indian sense, but similar to an Indonesian rijsttafel, or rice table, in which the dishes are spread out in a jewel-like array with the guests selecting among them. A chicken curry was the main event, but the "boys" were what made the dish for a condiment lover like me. I do not remember all of the eight condiments (or in fact if there were eight of them; there may have been ten), but they ranged from chopped peanuts to Major Grey's chutney. I do not remember the tastes of the food, only that they were richly varied and deeply satisfying and spoke to the creativity and exquisite culinary sensibility of the cook.

The preparation was an exercise in hospitality. Maya's cooking was a virtuoso performance that was part monologue and part dance routine, totally engaging and absolutely fascinating. There was a snippet of a song from a musical comedy at one point, a twist and a boogie at another, and a final flourish as a condiment was added. All was underscored by a running patter of anecdotes from her travels studded with information on the ingredients, commentary on the preparation, and descriptions of each dish. It was a whole new form of dinner theater: an entertainment calculated to astonish, amaze, and delight. Anyone who ever saw Maya in the kitchen knew that she loved cooking and adored entertaining—and she was damned good at it. I was captivated, and from then on remained in her thrall (albeit at a distance—flying too close to a flame can burn a moth).

Maya knew most of Sonoma, and they knew and respected her as well. After all, even though this was early in her literary career, it was after the publication of *I Know Why the Caged Bird Sings* had made her an international star and certainly a notable in the small village that Sonoma was in the 1970s. Then there was the fact that the take-no-prisoners fierce, six-foot-tall Black woman stood out in a crowd, commanded attention, and had become one of the area's leading lights.

Maya guided us through Sonoma. We journeyed to her various haunts in the area. One excursion was to Sebastiani Vineyards, where the Sebastianis were friends. The family patriarch was an old Italian winemaker of the kind that existed in the area before the "judgment of Paris" proclaimed California wines equal to those of France and made California wine country a tourist destination. We sampled and tasted, and I bought a bottle or two, but then he presented us with some bottles of his pet project—a wine called the Eye of the Swan. It was a New World variation that he'd crafted of the classic *oeil de perdrix* (eye of the partridge), which was a very special rose-pink champagne—a white made from black grapes, or *blanc de noir*, as that type of white wine is called in France. Sebastiani's swan's eye was glorious—lush and well-rounded with a salmon tinge. I bought a few more bottles and one came back to New York with me and lived in the back of my wine cupboard for several years.

One of the highlights of Sonoma for me was that I met Maya's mother, Lady (as she was called by everyone). I don't remember why she showed up or if we went to meet her somewhere, but one day, there she was. Lady surprised me; she was in many ways like my mother—except that my own mother didn't carry a loaded pistol in her bag. Lady was fierce and petite and exuberant, just like my mother; she was also a Capricorn like her, and we joked for a bit about goat-headed people and their stubbornness.

Sam and Lady had a particular affinity; he loved that she could finger-pop and bust a move with the best of them. He loved her joie de vivre, love of fine clothes, love of good food and ability to cook it, and her fondness for brown liquor, all of which he mirrored. I suspect that he also appreciated that her temper was as hair trigger as his own and perhaps even savored that she was completely unlike his own mother, Zula Floyd, the staid matriarch whom I'd met in Durham. One glance at Lady and you could clearly see the pentimento of the glamorous younger woman that she surely had been. She was dressed to the nines, and when she was ready to do something, she twirled on her high heels and, as she put it, "get her heels to clickin'" and headed off to conquer the world. It was easy to see where Maya got her fierce sense of self and her fearlessness.

Our visit to Sonoma included an obligatory stop in the San Francisco area. We left Paul and Maya for a day and headed down to the Bay Area, where Sam and I shared a meal at Mandarin, which had by then moved to Ghirardelli Square. The Chinese food served at Mandarin was exceptional, sophisticated, and tasty at a time when New York—indeed, the rest of the country—knew Chinese food only as a much Americanized version of Cantonese fare, quite unique. As I'd by then come to expect, Maya knew the owner, Cecilia Chiang, and had suggested the place as a must-see stop for San Francisco. Indeed it was.

The restaurant, which was on its way to becoming legendary, showcased the more complex tastes of Chinese food. It was one of the first places to serve Szechuan and Hunan cuisine, and the menu listed items such as hot-and-sour soup and pot stickers, as well as an astonishing minced squab that was served in lettuce-leaf containers. The decor was as amazing as the food. Located on the famous square with views of Alcatraz Island and Fisherman's Wharf outside the windows, it was like no other Chinese restaurant I'd ever seen. Not a dragon or phoenix was in sight; rather, it was an opulent palace with wood-beamed ceilings and decorated with Chinese antiques. Chiang, who was given to greeting customers at the door in a silk cheongsam adorned with jewelry from her extensive and very expensive collection, was as much a part of the lure of the place as the food. The three-hundred-seat restaurant was astonishingly elegant; the service was extraordinary, and the food tasted like nothing I'd ever had before. It set my bar for subsequent Chinese food quite high.

But this was a dinner excursion, so soon it was back to Maya's and our continuing round of visits to her friends in the surrounding area. We spent some time in Oakland with Maya's friend Jessica Truehaft (née Jessica Lucy Freeman-Mitford), one of Britain's Mitford sisters. She was the next to the last of the six daughters of the second Baron Redesdale who were a litmus test for the foibles and fantasies of the twentieth century. Nancy, the eldest, became an author and wrote *Love in a Cold Climate*, as well as biographies of historic figures like Louis XIV and Madame de Pompadour. Pamela was the least notorious and was referred to as "the rural Mitford." Diana was married to Sir Oswald Mosley, leader of the British Fascist party. The next youngest sibling, Unity, was even further to the right and a friend of Hitler and active in his social set. The youngest of the sisters, Deborah, known as Debo, became the dowager duchess of Devonshire.

Jessica—"Decca," as she was known to her friends—described their unorthodox childhood in *Hons and Rebels*. Decca hewed to the opposite end of the political spectrum from her siblings, became a member of the Communist party, and moved to America, where she worked as a reporter and journalist. Her investigation of the funeral industry, *The American Way of Death*, had been a best seller a decade before we drove down to spend the afternoon. I'm not sure where Maya and Decca met, but Decca had certainly been very active in the civil rights movement so it may have been that.

Awe was my main emotion for much of the trip to California, and certainly meeting one of the Mitford sisters (and the "cool" one at that) was the icing on the cake as far as I was concerned. I remember a warm welcome and much political conversation with in-crowd references that went over my head, although Jessica and I joked about sharing what was then an uncommon name. Most of all, I remember conviviality and an afternoon spent with people with a fierce love for language and rapier-fast wit trading conversation, opinion, and occasionally jokes in a California garden.

I had the invitation the next time that we traveled together: Sam and I journeyed to Haiti after I snagged a trip to the opening of the casino at the Royal Haitian Club, a spot that was created to lure tourists to the island. I was invited on an excursion to report on this casino, a trip that the government was sponsoring in an attempt to bolster tourism and usher in a new era of gambling on the island. The trip was notable because it was my first and only assignment related to gambling. I am absolutely not a gambler; I don't even play bingo and know no card game other than Old Maid, so Sam and I soon found a way to relax rules and spent our time hanging out with Nourry Menard, Paule Marshall's husband. He owned a soda company in Haiti that bottled the island's popular Kola Champagne and other drinks and spent some of his time there.

Nourry took us around Port-au-Prince, treating us to lunch at Le Rond Point, a downtown standby where we sampled items like *grillots de porc* (tasty garlic-infused pork bits served over white rice). We had the traditional *soupe aux pois rouges* (a red bean soup richly flavored with thyme) and salads dressed with a proper French vinaigrette. I'd been before on my earlier trip with Anna, so I knew that the food was traditional and delicious and that the capital's movers and shakers turned up for lunch, but eating there with Nourry was a special treat. We went to the Iron Market and the National Museum and generally acted like the tourists we were.

Sam, ever the avid golfer, even managed to find a golf course; I'm still not sure how, but we played a round on the course that had definitely seen better days. To this day, I can amaze golfers by recounting the nine-hole game that we played on what I jokingly referred to as Haiti's "browns" that day. (There was not a green blade of grass in sight.)

The New York disco the Hippopotamus had been transplanted to the nearby Habitation Leclerc, a luxury hostelry in a spot originally built for Napoleon Bonaparte's sister, Pauline, and so nights were spent boogying. With Nourry, we also discovered other aspects of Port-au-Prince nightlife; he knew the local spots and loved to dance. In New York and at the Habitation, it may have been about disco, but around the capital with Nourry, it was all about the merengue.

The merengue is a dance whose origin is disputed between Haiti and the Dominican Republic. (Legend has it that the dance was created in imitation of a shuffling peg-legged pirate.) The citizens of the two countries have an unbridled love of the merengue; it is just about the only thing that they can agree on, and folks from both places dance it with wild abandon. The Haitian upper crust danced at clubs like the Cabane Choucoune in Pétionville, where Port-au-Prince's *jeunesse dorée* gathered to shuffle feet and swing hips to the music's 2/4 rhythm. At the other end of the social spectrum, people got to swinging at Lambi in Carrefour, a blue-collar suburb of the capital. Lambi was an outdoor dance club on the water and it was decorated with conch shells (the "lambi" of its name) that were the detritus from the mollusks that were the main menu item. It was a huge psychic distance from the musky funk of Lambi to the French perfumes of the Cabane Choucoune, but in Pétion-ville and on the coast, the music blared nightly, and Sam and Nourry and I joined the folks who danced with the passionate delirium of those who knew that they were reveling on the volcano's edge and that change was coming.

All was lubricated with vast amounts of Rhum Barbancourt. So much rum was consumed that somehow, in the middle of playing a rousing game of craps on one of our obligatory casino visits, I must have taken off my eyeglasses. (Why, I do not know, because I'm tin-cup-and-a-dog blind without them.) In any case, I removed them and someone made off with them. I never saw them again. It certainly cemented my understanding of the term *blind drunk* and definitely upped my trust relationship with Sam, as I became dependent on him to shepherd me around as I wore my sunglasses like the blind fool I truly was. He kept my secret, and my eyeglass caper mercifully went unreported when I next saw Paule and company back in New York.

After each trip, we'd return to New York and to school and wait until the next break and try to figure out where to head next. Paris loomed. Like Rick and Elsa, we'd always have Paris, but unlike them, we'd never get to share time together in our favorite city. Rather, Sam went and stayed with Jimmy or I journeyed there solo, and we compared notes on our respective returns.

Although Sam and I did not spend time together in the

city, Paris remained the *belon* of my dreams. In other parts of Sam's life, as he discussed things with Jimmy and others, the names of many of the players, the dates, and the locales may have drifted over my head, but when it was about Paris, I understood. I usually managed to find my way through the maze of friendships and alliances thanks to my familiarity with French language and culture, my love of French food, and my knowledge of the city's Black cultural scene. Paris was a world where intelligence garnered respect and deep conversations were held nightly in cafés over several glasses of scotch or a *ballon* or two of rouge or in small bistros where the patron presided over the stove in the kitchen and Madame oversaw the front of the house. I still knew a few of them from my student days and discovered others.

While I'd stayed with my parents in the *quartiers populaires* on my first trip and spent a junior year abroad with a family in the snooty sixteenth arrondissement, I've always been a Left Bank girl in Paris. I've always been happiest near the Boulevard St.-Michel and the Boulevard St.-Germain on the south side of the Seine. Maybe it's a Black folks South Side thing, but that's the area I keep returning to, and it's the area I learned to love even more with Sam and Jimmy and their Parisian crew. At first, there were inexpensive hotels in the fifth arrondissement near the Boulevard St.-Michel, but as I became a bit more sophisticated and more flush with cash, I discovered the hotels on the Rue Jacob and near the Boulevard St.-Germain, where the Drugstore, a French version of an American-style all-purpose drugstore, loomed large.

The sixth arrondissement had traditionally been the haunt of American Blacks in Paris, who shared it with the French intelligentsia and beatniks who made the *caveaux de St. Germain-des-Près*, the underground jazz clubs of the neighborhood, the in-haunts in the 1950s. This was the neighborhood of Jean-Paul Sartre and Simone de Beauvoir, who roosted at the Café de Flore, and others who met regularly at Les Deux Magots and still others who lunched on the prix fixe menu at Petit Saint Benoit and ate with the literary crowd at the Brasserie Lipp.

The neighborhood was also a section of Paris that was renowned for its gay life and cruising spots. The gay club scene was going full blast, and it, too, was a part of Jimmy's world and therefore of Sam's Parisian one. Bernard Hassell, Jimmy's majordomo in St. Paul-de-Vence, was a former dancer at the Folies Bergère; he brought back to New York tales from the dance floors of various clubs. So although I never went, I'd certainly heard of Le Sept (7 Rue St. Anne), with its mirrored walls and multicolored lights and Le Fiacre (Rue St. Sulpice), Le Bilboquet, and other names bandied about in enough conversations to feel that I knew them. Le Palace opened with Grace Jones atop a pink Harley singing "La Vie en Rose" in March 1978, and the crowd decamped to the northern zones at night, but in the early years, it was all about St. Germain-des-Près.

My St. Germain-des-Près was a bit more sedate and centered on bookstores. La Hune and L'Ecume des Pages gobbled up my cash and weighted down my luggage. Flea markets yielded treasures, and reconnecting with friends and with my family from my junior year was a joy. It was also all about food. I was tasting my way through the inexpensive restaurants of the capital. Chez Guy offered Brazilian lunches where musicians offered samba and bossa nova and I could try out my skills as a percussionist shaking one of the pebble-filled soda cans they had at each table. Le Baobab presented Senegalese and other West African fare, and I could indulge in my love for *poulet yassa*. La Rhumerie took me back to the French Antilles with an obligatory *'ti* punch and some *acrats de morue*. My French meals tended to be of the bistro and brasserie type, and, unsurprisingly, a *choucroute* was obligatory on each trip. Then one year I was asked to meet up with Georges and Mary of my own infamous *choucroute* caper.

I certainly knew Georges was a chef held in great esteem by his American colleagues, and I knew that in Paris he was respected, even acclaimed. Before celebrity chefs were the rock stars of the culinary world, they were extraordinarily hardworking professionals whose names were known only to the cognoscenti. Georges's renown therefore was limited

to professionals in the culinary zone, and I had no idea of the French gastronomic heights that I'd scaled. I would find out just how wonderful a chef he was on one of my solo trips to Paris when he invited me to dine at Chez Garin.

My first impression of Chez Garin was burgundy—not the wine, the color, which was that of the upholstery of the supercomfortable chairs. The decor was old school of the type that the French call *feutré* (or felted), meaning that it is cossetting, comfortable. The pristine white napery was so well starched it could have been used instead of the well-sharpened knives that set the table, the heavy crystal gleamed, and the whole exemplified Baudelaire's *"luxe, calme et volupté."*

I was dining solo, but it was clear that I was a guest of the chef, and so I was ushered to a prime location. The meal began with *foie gras à la cuillère*, a dish in which the goose liver was sautéed and then transformed into a terrine; I slathered it on the toast that accompanied it, appreciating the unctuousness of creamy liver and delicacy of the seasonings. It was clearly yummy and a special presentation, but I'd had foie gras before and although I loved it, I was not astounded. I had expected Georges to be good, and he clearly was.

At the second course, I began to realize that this was a once-in-a-lifetime meal. I was presented with a small soup bowl of the type usually used to serve *soupe à l'onion grati-*

née. It was topped with puff pastry. When I pierced the flaky crust with my fork, the aroma was astonishing: savory with an underlying funk that I would learn came from the truffles that were the main ingredient. Indeed, the second course was a *ragout de truffes*—a truffle stew: huge chunks of pungent fresh black truffles served in a perfectly wrought brown sauce. It was rich—Lord, was it rich—and a revelation. I knew food could be very tasty and that some dishes could approach the sublime, but I had no idea that a dish could be a conversation of tastes and ideas. This was an ironic dish—a class war in a soup bowl that was as signifying as the monkey and as revolutionary as "La Marseillaise." The brown sauce was the nod to the peasant origins of the ragout, and the truffles—the sheer luxurious abundance of fresh truffles—were the pinnacle of gastronomic aristocracy. I indulged spooning up the sauce and learning the unfamiliar earthy pungency of fresh truffle. I tried but was finally defeated by the sheer richness of it all. I couldn't finish it and sent some of it back to the kitchen with abject apologies.

While I have regretted those returned truffles on many subsequent days, I am thrilled I did because if I hadn't, I would have never been able to complete the meal for which they had simply been a shot in the opening salvo. The next course was wheeled up on a mahogany trolley crowned with a silver rolltop. As the top of the trolley slid back, I was presented with the largest single piece of meat I'd ever seen at

that point: a saddle of lamb. Now, I knew legs, and racks of chops, and even crown roasts, but I'd never before met this big daddy of lamb cuts. The saddle was usually available only for two-person orders; I was being treated to an indulgence that I knew would be memorable and was also one of the specialties of the house. It was reverently sliced cross-wise, and I was presented with several perfectly pink slices accompanied by the vegetable infanticide that is a hallmark of la grande cuisine: tiny fresh vegetables the French call *les primeurs*, or first of the spring season. These were the thin verdant string beans that we now call *harciots verts*. There were *pommes dauphinoise*, the classic dish of thinly sliced potatoes, cream, butter, and garlic that had been cooked in a slow oven to a creamy crisp perfection. If that weren't enough, there was a purée of celeriac, butter, thick cream, and a hint of nutmeg. Georges, I would learn, was one of the first French chefs to serve vegetable purées as accompaniments. No knife was needed, and the tender lamb was beautifully yet simply seasoned and drizzled with a bit of jus. Despite my failings with the *ragout de truffes*, I managed to snuffle up the lamb, haricots verts, potatoes, and celeriac purée, savoring each morsel.

It didn't end there. This was a true French meal. The most splendid salad I'd ever tasted followed. Buttery lettuces were simply dressed with hazelnut oil and wine vinegar and tossed in a wooden bowl into which a garlic clove and a piece of the lamb's skin had been rubbed. The delicate lettuces had taken on just a hint of the garlic and the quintessence of lamb as though they, too, were remembering the previous course.

A cheese trolley followed featuring perfectly ripe chèvre, Port Salut, St. André, Gruyère, and more. By that time, Georges had finished with service and was circulating in the dining room. This was something he did often even though he was an old-school chef who was in the kitchen cooking. It was one of the first open kitchens, and Georges was notorious for hurling all manner of invective at his kitchen staff, much to the amusement of his regular clientele and to the despair of some newcomers. He sampled all of the wines before they were served to ensure their aptness, which more often than not also resulted in a rollicking atmosphere. As he often did with his regulars, he joined me at the table—a singular honor. I surprised Georges by savoring the cheese plate and demonstrating the scant but accurate knowledge that I'd acquired living with a French family. I settled on a bit of Roquefort, a strong cheese and one not expected to be liked by an American. Twinkling, he called for butter and a pear, which arrived tree ripe yet toothsomely crunchy, and proceeded to show me how Roquefort was eaten in some French families. He mashed some of the butter into the Roquefort, making it even creamier, and then slathered it on the crisp pear. Sublime. He must have noticed that my eyes were about to roll back in my head from sheer bliss combined with gluttony because dessert was deceptively simple, yet the perfect finish to this most indulgent meal: a quarter of sweet/tart ripe pineapple that served as palate cleanser and left me with a bit of sweetness in my mouth as an ending to the extraordinary meal.

I was too afloat on my wave of food sensations to be embarrassed at the time, but as days, and later months and years went by, I remembered the *choucroute garnie* I'd served him with growing horror. I'd offered unwashed sauerkraut, hot dogs, beer, and gin to the man who created that sublime meal. *Mortification* was not a strong enough word. Georges, it seemed, could have cared less. He'd accepted my gift as it was offered, mirroring an adage that I'd learned from my parents but that had been confirmed by Sam: when entertaining, always offer the best that you can afford and do not skimp. I had indeed done that. Georges understood my youth and my enthusiasm and appreciated the latter while indulging the former.

Some time later on another of my then-biannual trips to Paris, Georges and Mary paid me the ultimate compliment and invited me to their home. Georges must have been prepping at the restaurant, for I had lunch with Mary. I remember very little of the look of the apartment, only that it was traditionally French. What I do remember is meeting their beloved cat, Tikété. The feline's name meant "ticked" in

JESSICA B. HARRIS

French, and Abyssinian Tikété was a gorgeous beastie with
a triangular Egyptian-shaped head set atop a body of bur-
nished ticked fur and looked like a miniature tiger. Tikété
not only had full run of the house but ruled the roost with
an iron paw. Sam's Blues and Mouss and Askia, my two Siamese cats, were raised by Black folks and seriously trained
to remain out of the cooking areas and on the floor at meal-
time even if they were occasionally indulged with a morsel
or two. I was therefore astonished when Tikété leaped onto
the table and after a sniff and a peruse neatly circled himself
around the serving bowl of cauliflower that was the meat's
accompaniment. The cauliflower equally amazed me: it was
served whole and not broken into the florets that I was used
to. The whole looked like a still life: cat with "brain." I was
speechless.

The meal was delicious and proved that Mary was no
mean cook herself. That was only natural; she'd been dining
around the City of Light for years in the company of one
of its finest chefs and was a good friend of the man whose
culinary know-how helmed the iconic Time/Life series of
cookbooks. However, although I dined around New York
with Georges and Mary, we did not eat out elsewhere in
Paris other than at the sublime Chez Garin. I certainly did
not complain.

It was not all about food. Jimmy's generosity and my
French allowed me to go to the theater and understand, so

in January 1973, after a call from him to Tria French, his literary agent, I found myself in a central box seat at the Théâtre du Palais-Royal, watching a dress rehearsal for a new show. It featured another of Jimmy's friends, Benny Luke. I watched and waited for the three knocks that signal the beginning of a theatrical performance in France; then the curtain went up and out came Benny barefoot and wearing not much more than an apron and a jock strap, dusting and singing and sashaying. The play, *La Cage aux Folles*, wowed them in Paris, went on to spawn three movies, and then did another turn as a musical, but thanks to Jimmy and Tria French, who would be dead less than six months later, I could say that I'd been in the audience at the final dress rehearsal.

Our various Parisian sojourns were a part of the glue that cemented my relationship with Sam; we both seemed to need them to temper the day-to-day Queens College existence, with its papers and grades and exams and the rest. But soon enough we'd be hitting the road again to somewhere wonderful and filled with Sam's amazing friends.

Ten Boy Curry

There is no way I could even attempt to match the virtuoso performance that Maya Angelou put on when she prepared her curry for me in her Sonoma kitchen over four decades ago. My own curry, from my book Sky Juice and Flying Fish: Traditional Caribbean Cooking, *is more of a West Indian–type curry that includes potatoes along with the chicken. They serve to not only stretch the chicken, but also to lend substance to the curry. While this is traditionally eaten with roti, I like to serve it with rice (yes, I know two starches, but why not) and then add as many of the "boys"—mango chutney, tomato chutney, chopped peanuts, raisins, finely grated coconut, lime pickle, fresh pineapple pieces,* kachumber salad, raita, *and* papadum—*as I can get.*

– *Serves four to six* –

3 tablespoons butter
1 large onion, minced
4 garlic cloves, minced
2 teaspoons minced fresh ginger
3 tablespoons Madras-style curry
   powder
½ teaspoon crushed red chiles,
   or to taste

½ cup or more cane vinegar
3 pounds skinless, boneless
   chicken breasts cut into strips
3 large potatoes coarsely
   chopped

In a large frying pan, heat the butter and sauté the onion, garlic, and ginger until the onion is soft but not brown. Add the curry powder and the chiles, stirring so that they do not stick or burn. Add the vinegar. There should be enough to make a smooth paste. (If not, you may need as much as ¼ cup more.)

Cover the chicken pieces with the paste and place them in a covered bowl in the refrigerator. Allow the chicken pieces to marinate for at least 2 hours. When ready to cook, place the chicken pieces in a large frying pan and add enough water to reconstitute the paste and prevent scorching. Cover and cook over low heat for 30 minutes, checking occasionally. (You may find that you will have to add more water to prevent scorching.)

After 30 minutes, add the potatoes, cover, and continue to cook for an additional 15 minutes or until the chicken and potatoes are cooked through. Serve with white rice accompanied by the "boys."

Chapter Seven

TITINE AND TABASCO

The dappled sunshine and warm weather of the South of France beckoned us as it had Georges and Mary and Jimmy, who had arrived in St. Paul-de-Vence in 1970. Nice became the airport for all arrivals and departures. Located in the hills a little over nine miles from Nice, St. Paul-de-Vence is one of the *villages perchés*—the villages perched precariously on hilltops that cling to the sides for dear life and look as though a strong mistral could dislodge them and scatter their soft golden stones through the valleys and into the Mediterranean below. From the crenellated ramparts, views over the countryside dotted with orange, cypress, and olive trees and out to the sea are breathtaking.

The medieval village of St. Paul-de-Vence (usually known by its full name, as there are nine other St. Pauls in France) resonates for the French. Today it is a tourist mecca, a must-see stop on any visit to the Côte d'Azur. Local lore has it that the medieval hamlet was built at the insistence of Saint Paul, and indeed even in the eleventh century, it was known as Castrum Sancti Pauli. The medieval town was fortified in 1538 at the behest of King François I, who wanted to protect it from the incursions into Provence by Charles V of Spain. For centuries, the sleepy town, like its neighbors, was agricultural, growing olives, artichokes, roses, carnations, and oranges, but that began to change in 1911 when a tram was built to connect Cagnes-sur-Mer with Vence via St. Paul. Things developed further in the 1920s when artists Chaim Soutine, Raoul Dufy, and Paul Signac arrived and set up their easels. They were followed by others: Marc Chagall, who lived in neighboring Vence, and Pablo Picasso, who took up residence in Vallauris. They ushered in a golden age for the town that is noted for its beauty and has long been a touchstone in French history. A stroll through the twisting alleyways of the walled old town may reveal a small square with an ancient fountain or a garden brilliant with bougainvillea or a vista through an ancient archway out to the ultramarine waters of the Mediterranean on the horizon. And everywhere there are cats basking in sunny doorways: sleek beasties who seem to own the place and have become inextricably connected to it.

Today historic churches and museums attract day-trippers and Asian tourists even in the dead of winter. For art lovers, the village is a place of pilgrimage for the Fondation Maeght, the oldest museum of contemporary art in France, which boasts works by Joan Miró, Giacometti, Jean Arp, Marc Chagall, and other early-twentieth-century artists. For others, St. Paul has become an international destination because during World War II, when the area became an unoccupied free zone, the village became a mecca for writers, artists, and actors.

For lovers of the luxe life, St. Paul is known for its centerpiece *hostellerie* and restaurant La Colombe d'Or, an inn that has hosted the rich, the famous, and the infamous for more than three-quarters of a century. This village was where Jimmy had taken up residence in 1970, first in a hotel and later in a house he rented from a local woman named Jeanne Faure, a *pied noir* from Algeria with whom he had a stormy but lengthy friendship. She would eventually become one of his staunchest allies in the town and one of his protectors.

Sam had arrived before I did, and when I passed through customs at Nice airport to begin my stay, he was there to meet me. As usual, I'd come heavily ladened with my suitcase packed for every eventuality because I was scheduled to spend a week with Sam at Baldwin's home and I was rigid with apprehension and anticipation. A drive through vertiginous, twisting roads like the ones in the film *To Catch a Thief* is all I remember, along with some names on road signs that were familiar from a visit I'd made decades prior with my parents: St.-Laurent-du-Var, Cagnes-sur-Mer, Villneuve-Loubet, Biot. Soon we reached the house.

It's difficult to describe the house because it was actually several buildings with the typical plastered stone and red tiled roofs of the Provençal countryside, including a gatehouse at the entrance on the road in which Bernard Hassell, Jimmy's friend and self-appointed guardian, fittingly lived. A tall, lean former dancer, Bernard could be formidable and delighted in being terribly grand. In St. Paul, he was Baldwin's first line of defense: his friend, bodyguard, amanuensis, and Cerberus.

A stone walkway led from Bernard's roost to the main house, which was divided into two distinct living areas. The guest quarters where we were to stay were a combination bedroom–sitting room upstairs. Jimmy's completely separate apartment was downstairs: I would learn that he referred to it as his "torture chamber." Bernard, annoyed, I suspect, at the intrusion of a female not from the group into his domain, was initially less than welcoming, but all was smoothed over by Sam, who took me to get settled. I waited and unpacked my luggage.

Baldwin never lost his African American palate and, I had been informed, loved hot sauce that he could not get in France. (Tabasco would not do.) I'd been instructed that this would be the most welcome gift I could bring Jimmy, and so the most precious items in my suitcase were two huge bottles of Red Devil Hot Sauce. With the inevitability of fate, one shattered, and I spent the rest of the extraordinary week rinsing glass shards and red pepper out of my clothes.

I'd met Jimmy briefly in New York on a few occasions, and I certainly knew of the great affection that he and Sam had for each other. (Sam called him "Jimmy" and he called Sam, teasingly, "Sammy," a lèse-majesté Sam would have permitted no one else but one that he loved, for it signaled their special relationship.) This, though, was different; I was at Jimmy's home and he was relaxed and at rest, albeit a rest that was all about work. It was a view of Baldwin few saw, and I was very aware of the singular honor it bestowed.

Soon enough, Jimmy arrived: febrile, intense, and terrifyingly impressive. By this time, Baldwin's visage has become so iconic that its familiarity was startling, but there he was in the flesh. Then he smiled—oh, that smile; it lit up his entire being and revealed not only his huge capacity for joy but also the hurt that lay just beneath the skin. It was a knowing smile, a wise smile, a smile of welcome with immense generosity for the naive, out-of-my-depth young woman that I was. He led us to a table set out among the towering cypress trees where lunch had been set, which Jimmy would later refer to as his welcome table, referring to the old spiritual. The meal was simple: loaves of crusty French bread, a red wine from the region (probably a Bandol), and a tureen filled with a hearty *soupe au pistou* prepared by Valerie Sordello, Baldwin's housekeeper and cook. Baldwin ate, chatted, and then vanished.

I would learn that Baldwin disappeared during the day down to his torture chamber. He composed on yellow pads, but by the time I arrived, he was working on his final edits, and so the sound of the typewriter could be heard. When things were going well, it was a steady sound; when it stopped . . . it was noticed. He reappeared for lunch and for cocktails, dinner, and whatever was going on in the evening before descending again. Often in the evening, his appearance signaled a trip up the hill to La Colombe d'Or, the old section of town.

Originally a café with three rooms called Chez Robinson in the 1920s, it was run by Paul Roux, a farmer turned café owner who eventually became a hotelier, and his wife, the legendary Baptistine, better known as Titine. The place grew and by 1932, it was large enough to merit a more serious name. They baptized it La Colombe d'Or for the doves that roosted nearby and had become the inn's totems. The inn and restaurant quickly became a hangout for the artists who were making the hills above Nice an artists' haven. An art lover, Roux traded art for food, and soon works by Picasso, Léger, Matisse, Rouault, and others began to hang on the walls of the restaurant.

The artists were part of the first wave of creative folks

to arrive in St. Paul-de-Vence and were soon followed by a *beau monde* of writers and actors. Charlie Chaplin, Josephine Baker, Colette, and more signed the guest books. The names Jacques Prévert, Gérard Philipe, and Marcel Pagnol may be less familiar to the non-Francophile, but the names Jean-Paul Belmondo and Marcello Mastroianni and Frank Sinatra and Sammy Davis Jr. explain the inn's mystique to the world. Yves Montand and Simone Signoret were married there. By 1973, the hotel had hosted just about everyone known or trying to be known in the Western world; sooner or later they all came to La Colombe d'Or.

Baldwin lived down the road on the Chemin du Pilon, and it was his habit to head up to the inn for a preprandial drink and to catch up on the news of the town that he had adopted as his own and that had adopted him. The small, narrow bar was his preferred roost, and he'd hunker down on one of the three-legged stools to break his day from the downstairs torture chamber with the first Johnnie Walker of the evening.

When Baldwin arrived in St. Paul in 1970, Titine became his protector and Gallic godmother. She was by then the doyenne of the town, and a word from her meant instant acceptance; she protected him and guarded him with the ferocity of a mother tigress. Jimmy said of her in his last interview,

Titine Roux was the old lady that ran *La Colombe d'Or*, which is a world-famous restaurant and inn. She became my guardian. I never lived in a small town before, which is not easy, and she protected me. I could come in and lunch at her restaurant. And I didn't realize it at first that she had picked herself to be my protector.

By 1973, Titine was no longer running the hotel: it had been passed on to her children, but she was still a formidable presence, and her role as Jimmy's protector was firmly in place. Crow-like in her black dress with opaque black cotton stockings, she looked very much like any other Mediterranean grandmother leaning on her cane. In her world of St. Paul-de-Vence, and increasingly in that of France, the plump doyenne of the hotel enjoyed a fame equal to Jimmy's and she was equally terrifying until you noticed her bemused gaze at the world expressed through her twinkling eyes. She liked me; I suspected it was my speaking French. She'd decided that Sam and I made a great couple and would tease us, always asking when would we get married, no doubt relishing Sam's discomfort and my delight. She was at ease with the famous who flocked to her hotel and made sure that those she favored were also at ease.

One night, we headed up the hill as usual, but when we got to the door of the bar, I stopped stupefied, rendered speechless by the presence on the other side of the archway. Jimmy and Sam went on through, and Jimmy greeted the individual facing us with, "Bonsoir, Yves. Where's Simone?" Sitting in one of the bar's corners was Yves Montand, he of the mellifluous voice whose renditions of "La Mer" and "Autumn Leaves" had made more than one generation swoon. He'd been discovered by none other than Edith Piaf, had been her lover, and had a notorious affair with Marilyn Monroe. He was known worldwide. The Simone referred to was Simone Signoret, his wife, who combined beauty with a prodigious intellect and spoke French, German, and English. She was the first French actress to win a Best Actress Oscar and had even inspired Nina Simone's stage name. I was staggered and starstruck. We joined him at the small table and after babbling *bonsoir*, I said not another word for the evening, unsure of what idiocy I might utter.

Montand was the unofficial mayor of St. Paul. His games of *boules* with such French stars as Serge Reggiani, Henri Salvador, and Lino Ventura on the square in front of the Café de la Place were the stuff of local legend. Montand, Signoret, and Baldwin were friends; they shared the complicity of the extremely famous, each understanding just what "the price of the ticket" was. Montand and his wife would spend hours at La Colombe d'Or chatting with Jimmy about the world, politics, and life. That night, though, Signoret was at home with a cold; her sniffles probably saved me from a major social gaffe, for I'm not sure if I could have handled that much star power. I would not meet her that summer, but nonetheless my week chez Jimmy in St. Paul-de-Vence tested my social abilities to the maximum, but they'd been tested before in Durham, and I passed both times.

Jimmy liked excursions and adored good company. As much as he required solitude and never missed his daily appointment in the torture chamber, he also liked diversions and reveled in the presence of folks who had good conversation. He possessed, as did many of the circle of friends, an incredible ability to stay out, hang out, drink well and often, and never miss his downstairs date. His work ethic was astounding. Even after an evening of carousing and discussing all manner of things from chalk to cheese, he would head downstairs again, and soon the pecking of the typewriter would be heard. He'd be back at work. Whatever the diversion, sooner or later, it was all about the work, always about the work. It ruled him and his life as it ruled them all.

By the time of my visit, Jimmy was not only an international legend but a star in his own right in St. Paul: a fixture at La Colombe d'Or and invited to all of the activities of the artists' colony that the area had become. One evening, we dressed up in summer finery and headed off to a party at César's, another one of his friends.

César Baldaccini never used his last name. In St. Paul, you only had to say "César" and everyone knew whom you meant. He'd arrived in the region in the 1960s from his native Marseilles, part of a newer wave of artists, and established himself as one of the more important artists of the period. The man of the compressions, as he was then called, first became known in the 1960s as one of the founders and the stars of the *nouveau réalisme* movement. He was noted for sculptural works assembled from compressed cars, motorcycles, and the detritus of the modern consumer society. He cast in bronze and created sculptures like those that greeted visitors to La Colombe d'Or, and his public art was seen in town squares throughout the country. He is especially revered in France as the creator of the statuette that is given out at the Film Festival at Cannes; it is simply known as the César in the same way that the Motion Picture Academy's awards are called the Oscar.

César was a bon vivant of the old school. Someone once referred to him as seeming to be a character out of a work by Marc Pagnol, whose trilogy, *Fanny*, *Marius*, and *César*, defined Provence for many. Indeed, his Marseilles accent, complete with rolling *r*'s, his artistic exuberance, and his joie de vivre made him seem like a throwback to another era. With a graying beard and the unkempt look of a pet brown bear, and an oh-so-Gallic way of wearing paint-stained shirts, corduroy trousers, and clogs, he was almost a caricature of a French artist. He loved life and had a playful way that was contagious. This I sensed from the minute we crossed the threshold into his home.

His home was a Côté Sud fantasy of his own work and the work of other artists like that of his friend and sometimes rival, Arman. Antique and modern furniture jostled for position; the ordinary and the exotic sat side by side, and there was even room for kitsch like the peculiar style of shards of glass and mirror and crockery embedded in plaster and concrete known in France as *pique assiette*. This was my first peek at the artistic French Provençal style that spawned its own design revolution. I recall outdoor lights in the garden and a Rabelaisian amount of food. Elegant French country women with perfectly tousled and sun-streaked blonde hair and gentlemen in white linen trousers and feet shoved sockless into expensive loafers gathered with others whose affect was more artistic; women of a certain age with real jewelry and artists with paint-stained fingers all circulated. My French again stood me in good stead; I could keep up with the badinage, make conversation, and even catch some of the political allusions. I had an intense conversation with César's lady, an exquisitely elegant woman with prematurely white hair; she was casually dressed in the bohemian chic that the French do so well. I don't remember the topic of our conversation, but I do recall an affinity and that I garnered a return invitation whenever I was back in the region.

Baldwin was greeted not as a celebrity, but as a St. Paul local: one of the band of artists and writers who had found and made this corner of France their refuge. This was another of his circles of friends—one he'd established away from the land of his birth but one that also accepted him as their own. No stranger in the village here, he fit in with the international intellectual crew of artists as much as he fit in at the lecture podium, the pulpit, at Mikell's, or among the crowds at El Faro. It was the face of another of the multiple individuals who lived within Baldwin and whom he referred to as "all of those strangers"—another facet of his complex life.

The days in St. Paul were simple and rhythmed by Baldwin's writing schedule. There were walks up the hill into town to stop at the Café de la Place for a drink and watch the men out front play endless games of Provence's national sport, *boules*. During these interludes, I learned that the game is accurately called *pétanque*, and it is played with *boules*, as the balls are called in a *boulodrome*, which is basically any dirt terrain flat enough to allow for the pitch to be established. It's a simple game but can be played with the intensity of chess by the initiated. It calls for skill, accuracy, and judgment—dare I say cunning—virtues that are held dear by every Provençal peasant. Watching as the shooters attempted to place their *boules* closest to the *cochonnet*, as the target is called, I mused that it was nothing more than a game of marbles with bigger marbles and bigger boys. But I understood how it could be a major spectator sport, especially if viewed from the sunny terrace of a café while sipping a pastis or a glass of rosé de Provence.

In the walled city, there were galleries to be visited and there were occasional excursions to a nearby town. There was the Fondation Maeght to explore as well, but in truth, La Colombe d'Or was the center of life away from chez Jimmy. Apart from the evening drinks and the occasional meal, it was the center of the life of what still essentially remained a village, albeit a village of notables and famous. The bar beckoned and the restaurant interior defined quiet luxury with its dark wood wainscoting and its walls hung with artwork acquired from the major artists of a generation.

Nice, with its Cour Saleya market, also beckoned and offered strolling. Sam and I shared the cooking gene, so just investigating the varieties of produce, array of olives, and varieties of olive oil was inspiring. There were always more cafés to discover and time for sitting, reading, catching up on conversations, and simply savoring the lavender- and orange blossom–scented air and the beauty of the countryside that is the back country of Nice. Days were punctuated with wonderful meals of Provençal classics that used the freshest bounty from nearby markets. Baldwin's housekeeper, Valerie, proved herself a most adept cook, preparing classic dishes from the Provençal regional repertoire, although I had not ventured professionally into that culinary domain in any real way at that time. When I did, I had sense memories of her *boeuf en daube*, aioli, and ratatouille to guide me.

The week was not all resting and parties and outings.

One evening, after dinner had been eaten and all was finished, Jimmy invited Bernard, Sam, and me downstairs. He'd made popcorn the old-fashioned way, with a heavy pot, oil, and shaking as the corn popped. It was a special treat to accompany his reading of the text that he'd been working on: a novel. We trooped downstairs, and I got to see the torture chamber. It was a large room with an enormous fireplace with photographs and other keepsakes organized in professorial disarray on the mantelpiece; it was furnished spartanly with a bed and a writing table and a desktop on which the typewriter sat majestically. We took up our positions in chairs, on the bed, and on the floor, and popcorn was distributed. I noticed that I was seated near Jimmy, so that he seemed to be reading directly to me. He began:

> *I look at myself in the mirror.* I know that I was christened Clementine, and so it would make sense if people called me Clem, or even, come to think of it, Clementine, since that's my name: but they don't. People call me Tish.

The tale spilled onward, the haunting story of Tish and Fonny that would be the novel *If Beale Street Could Talk.* Baldwin read from the opening scene of Tish telling the incarcerated Fonny that she is pregnant with his child. He read on and on, all of the pages of the hand-typed manuscript. The evening turned into night, and night to incipient dawn, and Baldwin read on. He read the entire story, all of the harrowing tale of Fonny's incarceration and Tish's attempts to free him, and throughout it all Baldwin had me affixed in his laser beam gaze. With the dawn came the ending:

> Fonny is working on the wood, on the stone, whistling, smiling. And from far away, but coming nearer, the baby cries and cries and cries and cries and cries and cries and cries and cries, cries like it means to wake the dead.

I was mesmerized when he asked what I thought; I could only reply, "Amazing, astonishing." The answer was accepted graciously. It didn't seem to completely satisfy, but it was all I could offer.

Toward the end of my week, Baldwin's house again became a flurry of activity because Toni Morrison was going to arrive and Angela Davis might be showing up a few days after that. The sleeping arrangements were rejigged, allowing me to say that I shared a bedroom with Toni Morrison. I knew her from my work as a book review editor and burgeoning feature writer at *Essence* magazine, where I'd later interview her.

Jimmy made popcorn again, and we all trooped downstairs for the second time in a few days. Again Jimmy read the entire manuscript. Again the harrowing story of unjust incarceration was told. Again the evening folded into the morning as the story unwound. This time, though, Jimmy fixed the laser beam of his concentration on Morrison. At the end of the second reading, he asked the same question of Morrison that I had been unable to answer satisfactorily. What did she think? How was it? Infinitely wiser than I and trained as an editor, Morrison immediately understood the multiple levels of the question and the situation. She answered with remarks about the point of view and the handling of the female voice, agreeing that it did work. The unspoken question had been answered. The lightbulb finally dawned for me. The book was almost completed, and Baldwin was looking for comments about the accuracy of the female voice that he had selected as a vehicle for telling the tale. It was a conversation of equals, with respect for each other's work and trust in each other's judgment.

I'd recognized that the story was connected with the real-life story of William Anthony "Tony" Maynard: a twentieth-century horror story that resonates equally in the twenty-first. As recounted in the *New York Post* of October 23, 1973, by James Wechsler, then that newspaper's editorial director, "Maynard was a 31-year-old aspiring actor, theatrical agent, civil rights activist and friend of such figures as William Styron and James Baldwin when he was suddenly jailed in the senseless predawn killing of a marine sergeant in Greenwich Village." The article presents the case: two

previous prosecutions had resulted in hung juries, two of the
five judges in the Appellate Division found "grievous preju-
dicial errors in the conduct of the trial that led to his convic-
tion," and an eyewitness questioned by the police offered a
description "utterly at variance with Maynard's."

Baldwin had written about it in *No Name in the Street*
in 1972, detailing the Kafka-esque intricacies of the case.
He defines Maynard as his bodyguard, chauffeur, and man
Friday—a role similar to that later taken over by Bernard
Hassell. Maynard was undeniably Baldwin's friend, and the
case had become a cause célèbre for Baldwin, who worked
with Maynard's sister Valerie to secure his release. *No Name
in the Street* is his cri de coeur—his white-hot rage. The work
that he had read to us in the summer of 1973 while peering
into my soul was another version of the story: a fictionalized
one that railed equally at the horrors confronted by Black
and Puerto Rican people caught up in American justice:

> Black and Puerto Rican matrons, black and Puerto Rican
> girls, black and Puerto Rican boys, black and Puerto
> Rican men: such are the fish trapped in the net called
> justice.

He'd said that in *No Name in the Street*. In *If Beale Street
Could Talk*, he showed what it felt like with a different, perhaps softer spin.

In *If Beale Street Could Talk*, the fictionalized story of Tony Maynard, Clementine, known as Tish, who narrates the story, is a twenty-something Black woman—my age at the time. The book is written from the point of view of that young woman who could have under other circumstances been me. Morrison understood that as well and said what I could not. *If Beale Street Could Talk* would be published the following year to mixed reviews—a disappointment for Baldwin, but one mitigated by Maynard's release in the fall of 1973. I would always regard it with special respect because I knew the "secret" of how I had heard it from Baldwin's mouth in the room in which it had been written . . . twice.

I would later meet Maynard at Sam's apartment in New York. He was tall and lean and handsome, with the kind of good looks that should set off clanging warning bells signaling trouble but never do. Sullen and very much the reluctant focus of the attention that he was given, he was fêted and celebrated by Sam and the crew. I noticed that he was wearing jewelry that I had given Sam. I wasn't amused but had learned to keep my "bourgeois" thoughts to myself and so held my peace. Maynard proved a disappointment to Baldwin and showed no interest in remaining the focus of his savior's ministrations.

But in St. Paul, Tony was a fictionalized character. In those halcyon days, names mentioned and understood by all but me in the shorthand of friendship presaged folks I'd met or would later meet in Paris or in New York or learn of from other circumstances: Benny Luke, Tria French, Lucien Happersberger, Richard Marek, and more. These were names of friends and dear ones and colleagues, and I would learn their importance to Jimmy's life and work. He also had legions of friends and admirers up and down the Mediterranean coast, but perhaps none was dearer to him than Mary Painter.

Mary Painter and Georges had retired from Paris to Solliès-Toucas to open a restaurant called Le Lingousto. The small town in the hills above Toulon was another side of Provence and was also home to Richard Olney, general editor of the Time/Life series of cookbooks. Paul and Julia Child had settled nearby as well at the behest of Simca, her coauthor. Something about the air of Provence seemed to draw all manner of folk to it in the early years of the twentieth century's eighth decade. If St. Paul-de-Vence was all about work and relaxation, Solliès-Toucas was about friendship, fun, and food. Our motley band would spend an unforgettable day visiting them there.

One morning a car was procured and we headed off to visit Georges and Mary. We threaded our way through the twisting roads among the olive and orange trees down out

Sam to the Costa del Sol. My parents had a time-share there. If the time with Jimmy was the seal on our life as a couple, Spain was like playing house or playing honeymoon. There was great food. There were late-night dinners in Torremolinos, upstairs at Perdro's on the main drag; the place specialized in tableside service, and the steak au poivre was a fork-tender delight. Easo's on the Torremolinos/Marbella road offered sublime gazpacho and *cinco pescados andaluz*. We ate sardines grilled on skewers on the beach, where the sand was too hot to walk on. There were rounds of golf and even a hole in one that I hit. I honestly didn't know where the ball had gone, but Sam's glee in the shot and the ball in the cup at the end of the walk to the green were a triumph that seemed to cap our stay and make it all fairy-tale perfect. There was more gazpacho and more golf and more days spent exploring the restaurants and beaches, but delightful as they were, nothing could quite beat the allure and the delight of St. Paul-de-Vence and the specialness of having been with Jimmy *chez lui*—in the intimacy of his home on the periphery of the intimacy of the confidence he had for Sam.

They were heady times indeed. Nothing could survive that white-hot intensity, and neither could our relationship. It ended not with a bang but with the ebbing of a wave that had reached its crescendo and was flowing back out to sea. We headed to other places and met other people. I matured steadily, was less tolerant of offenses and slights real or imagined, and moved on to other things. But love never really dies, and the affection that Sam and I had for each other also evolved and morphed. We saw each other at school and indeed often off campus and were still an occasional couple when I had an extra ticket to something or Sam wanted a companion. We drifted apart, coming to a fork in the road and separating paths, yet we always maintained a kinship, friendship, and a complicity about the world that we had shared for a time.

Soupe au Pistou

Any meal with James Baldwin was bound to be unforgettable, but my first meal in St. Paul-de-Vence, outside under the tall cypress trees at Jimmy's house, is one that lives in my head, heart, and taste buds more than forty years later. The outdoor dining room centered around what I would later learn he called his welcome table. The summer day boasted the cerulean blue sky of the sort that is produced only in Provence and the air was fragrant with the heady mix of citrus, lavender, and sea that is the region's hallmark scent. The meal was a Mediterranean classic: soupe au pistou. This soup will always mean Jimmy and Sam and that wondrous week to me.

– Serves four to six –

1 large leek (white and pale green parts only), scrubbed and thinly sliced
1 celery rib, cut into ½-inch pieces
1 large carrot, cut into ½-inch pieces
1 garlic clove, minced
1 large sprig of thyme
2 tablespoons extra-virgin olive oil
½ teaspoon salt
¼ teaspoon pepper
½ pound boiling potatoes, peeled and cut into ½-inch pieces
¾ pound kale, coarsely chopped
½ pound zucchini, cut into ½-inch pieces
½ pound string beans, trimmed and cut into 1-inch pieces
¾ cup medium elbow pasta shells

Cook the leek, celery, carrot, garlic, and thyme in oil in a 5- or 6-quart heavy pot with ½ teaspoon of salt and ¼ teaspoon of pepper over medium heat, stirring occasionally, until the vegetables brown, about 5 minutes.

Add the potatoes and cook, stirring occasionally, until they begin to soften, about 5 minutes. Add 8 cups of water and bring to a boil, stirring and scraping up any brown bits. Stir in the kale, zucchini, string beans, pasta, and salt to taste. Simmer, uncovered, until the pasta is al dente and the vegetables are tender, about 10 minutes. Discard the thyme and adjust the seasoning.

Remove the soup from the heat, stir in half of the *pistou*, and adjust the seasoning to taste. Serve hot with the remaining *pistou* stirred in as desired.

Pistou

Makes about 2 cups

1 small tomato
1 cup packed basil leaves
½ cup packed flat-leaf parsley
  leaves
2 garlic cloves, minced

2 tablespoons extra-virgin
  olive oil
3 ounces Gruyère cheese,
  coarsely grated

Core the tomato, then purée it with the basil, parsley, and garlic in a food processor. Slowly drizzle in the oil, add the cheese, and blend well.

Chapter Eight

SOUL-FULL

The world was changing. My world was changing. It was a time of men in Cuban-heeled boots and peacock-hued finery. It was a time of doors opening to closets and doors closing on lies, both intentional and inadvertent. It began as a time of famous clubs like Studio 54 and other venues less savory, like the Continental Baths, where Bette Midler and Barry Manilow had their starts amid the toweled gay crowd and avant-garde. I never made it to either of them, but knew many folks who were regulars at each.

Toward the river that was not that far from my West Village apartment were more notorious venues like the Ramrod on West Street, Badlands nearby on Christopher Street, and the Anvil at the end of Fourteenth Street. The notorious Mineshaft was located at 835 Washington Street around the corner from Sam's house. It was considered the most hard-core of the unsavory Meatpacking District's S&M clubs. There, impersonal sex and "glory holes," a golden shower tub, and other over-the-top reveling in the newfound gay sexual freedom were evidenced nightly. I skirted the perimeters of these places, dimly aware of them and understanding little of the shorthand of my gay friends who spoke of them in front of me with knowing nods and lowered voices.

In the beginning, there was no hint of the fast-arriving plague years: the times that would signal the end of an era. Then, in 1981, the underground network of information began to spread talk of a type of pneumonia that affected homosexuals. By 1982, the word had spread, as had the illness, which was given a name, AIDS (acquired immune deficiency syndrome). The term replaced GRID (gay-related immune deficiency), as it was discovered that the illness affected not only gay men but also intravenous drug users, hemophiliacs, and, for some reason, Haitians. That year it was determined that the illness could also be transmitted by blood transfusions. By 1984, the retrovirus that caused the illness was isolated, and the world became familiar with HIV. The plague years were fully upon us.

By 1986, there was widespread panic: a sore that didn't heal or a fever blister in the wrong place could signal the end of a relationship and the beginning of a journey down dark and unexplored corridors that could leave scars that would result in inconclusive tests and often a ten-year waiting period with a death sentence hanging over your head. It was a time of uncertainty and difficulty. Safe sex was urged; condoms became commonplace. AIDS crept onto the scene slowly, at first a looming spectre that lurked in the cobblestoned streets and dim alleyways. We all learned about Kaposi's sarcoma and pneumocystic pneumonia. Rock Hudson died of AIDS in 1985 and Ricky Wilson of the B-52's succumbed the same year.

Living in the West Village, I was at the epicenter of it all, albeit on the periphery. Slowly but with the inexorability of fate, it entered our lives. There were rumors and tales and talk. Once when the discussion had turned to what had become known as "safe sex," Baldwin opined that there was no such thing: sex had always been dangerous and there was no more danger than ever before. It was an interesting perspective. I thought of it and of how it really didn't quite capture the new fear that I saw in the eyes of my other gay friends. Living in the West Village, I watched as their lives changed and as they became pariahs in the world they had only just claimed as their own. Gay I knew about. I lived a life tangential to the arts and reveled in the company of actors, artists, writers, dancers, and more. I had, after all, gone to the High School of Performing Arts and sat next to Teddy, a dance student, who wore bright blue eye shadow in biology class. I counted myself as reasonably sophisticated. I knew more than most of the members of the Saturday-night sinners and had myriad friends who loved to push social envelopes in multiple ways. They challenged. They fought. They were the avant-garde of a new social and sexual consciousness whose behavior placed them squarely in the crosshairs of the coming scourge.

I adored the arts and was tangential to theater folk and so knew many gay men and had more than a few close gay friends. There was Darrell—my Asian brother—my travel-writing colleague and sometimes mentor. We'd met on a press trip to Zambia and had recognized each other as neighbors in the Village when we both referred to the neighborhood deli as "Tiffany's" for its astronomical prices. I'd certainly known he was gay; we'd joked about how a gay man from Salt Lake City, Utah, could make it in New York. We were fast friends, and one birthday he'd surprised me with the gift of a gorgeous jade fish and a card that read, "For the Chinese, jade is the cement that bonds friendship." We were kindred spirits with the keys to each other's apartments so that we could take on cat-feeding duties when one of us was out of town. I'd met several of his partners and was pleased when he seemed to have found a permanent link, even if his new partner had truly shocked me on one notable occasion by answering the door wearing a brightly hued Pucci ensemble and full makeup and looking better in it than I could have. Then one day Darrell called me in a panic and asked me to accompany him to the emergency room. I did, and as we waited on the impersonal plastic benches, I could sense his inner turmoil. He needed nothing more than palliative care for a nonfatal ailment. Darrell was fine that time, but a few years later, they buried him clutching his teddy bear. His parents from Salt Lake City didn't know what had hit them.

There was Patrick Kelly—my wonderfully crazy friend from Vicksburg, Mississippi, who took on the world and transformed his grandmother's button box into a fashion empire. I'd met Patrick in New York through my friend Elaine Evans, a hairdresser. We clicked on a mutual love of luxury brands. He remains the only man other than my father to give me a Hermès scarf, and I gave him a Loewe agenda. We giggled together and exchanged recipes and I was one of the last people to buy the clothing that he then sold in ensembles he called "groups" before he decamped to Paris in 1979. He left me with a bottle of the Evening in Paris perfume that we both remembered buying for our mothers in long-forgotten five-and-ten stores, and I treasured the small, tasseled cobalt blue bottle.

In Paris, Patrick spread his wings and took the world by storm, infusing French fashion with his own down-home brand of humor. He fried chicken and served it at his early shows, decorated his showroom with black dolls and golliwogs, and appeared in baggy overalls with his trademark red, white, and blue Paris cap. He was in France building his business and becoming the first American and the first Black to gain admittance to the prestigious Chambre Syndicale du Prêt à Porter des Couturiers et des Créateurs de Mode. He avoided AIDS in New York City, but like the man in the biblical parable, had his appointment in Paris and succumbed to the disease there.

There was Lowell Todd, Sam's neighbor who stepped into the role of my big brother. Lowell had worked for the board of education and had left it all to become a cabaret musician. He lived across from Sam on Horatio Street in a small apartment where the upright piano on which he practiced endlessly seemed to be the only piece of furniture. Lowell prided himself on his resemblance to and friendship with Bobby Short, and he sort of looked like him in all but the piano playing. Lowell was teaching himself to play the piano and had learned the chord progressions for his jazz and cabaret offerings, but at times the renditions were a tad labored. Somehow, though, Lowell got gigs at various small restaurants around the Village. I went to one fairly regularly and kidded him that he should play "Satin Doll" whenever

I entered. Sweet man that he was, he indulged me, although sometimes the chords were not always those that would have been recognized by the Duke. I loved the acknowledgment, and for a while I reveled in that minimal notoriety for the duration of his run at that restaurant. Lowell was a quiet constant. He was also my protector and often ran interference with Sam. Once, I called him frantically when a bottle exploded in my kitchen, and I found myself looking down at an open wound that revealed my ankle bone.

Lowell didn't show up. Instead he called Sam, who arrived and rode in the ambulance with me the few blocks around the corner to St. Vincent's, our neighborhood hospital. There, we were met with all of the skepticism emblematic of the inherent racism in the hospital system. A Black couple arriving with something that clearly was a wound from broken glass brought raised eyebrows and the unspoken subtext of domestic violence. For once, thank goodness, Sam was quiet and let his concern for me override his desire to tell off the smirking intern who read a whole different story into the accident.

The accident, though, proved what I somehow intuited: although we'd not been a couple for several years, Sam was and would always be there for me in his way. He was there when my father died in 1985. The memorial service marked his first time back in my parents' house in a while, and I recall him on the back porch at the subsequent repast surrounded by the adoring audience of folk he still always drew and regaling them with tales of my father.

In the aftermath of my father's death, we again lost track of each other. Our relationship had dwindled down to a thing of affection and friendship and of occasional meetings broken by long periods of seeing each other only at school. In the fall of 1985, he wasn't there. I now suspect that he'd absented himself from school on either a sabbatical or sick leave. I was therefore a little surprised when he called me in early 1986 to ask me out to dinner. I'm not sure if it was a birthday treat for our Piscean February/March birthdays or just a let's-get-together-and-catch-up dinner, but delighted to hear from him, I accepted.

Celebrating our mutual love of things French, we decided on Quatorze, a French bistro on Fourteenth Street not too far from our apartments, and set the time. Since our last meeting, my first book, *Hot Stuff: A Cookbook in Praise of the Piquant*, had come out and I took him a copy. I inscribed it, "To Sam, You knew I had it in me before I knew I had it in me." He was delighted with the book and thrilled at the inscription, crowing about just how accurate it was. Dinner progressed without incident. The food was wonderful; I'm pretty sure I had the *choucroute*, which had become a culinary theme in our relationship.

The wait staff performed without incurring Sam's wrath.

It was like old times, with none of the fits of rage and accusations that had marred our latter years. All of our chemistry was at full bubble, and for a nod or a gesture, we'd have probably fallen back into bed and into our old routine, but somehow we did not. Restraint was never our thing, so I guess that should have been the first hint that something profound had shifted. Something was up. The evening would have been a perfect first date; it was equally memorable as a last one.

Lowell was the one who called. He was brief and cryptic: "Sam's in St. Vincent's!"

"What? I just saw him a few weeks ago. I'll go over and see him." I headed over to Saint Vincent's, a five-minute walk from my apartment. It took all I could muster; I am a hospital coward and hate going to them because my father had agonized in and out of hospitals for a decade before dying at home less than a year before.

St. Vincent's Hospital was located at the corner of West Twelfth Street and Seventh Avenue. I'd been there with Darrell, and I'd been there with Sam when I cut my leg a few years prior. The hospital had been founded in 1849 and was one of the few charity hospitals in the city. It treated the surviving victims of the *Titanic* sinking and of the Triangle Shirtwaist Factory fire, and Edna St. Vincent Millay was named for the institution after it saved her uncle's life. The building occupied the city block on which it stood: stolid, massive, and, seemingly indestructible—a comfort to those who turned to it in times of need. In the 1980s, Saint Vincent's housed the first and largest AIDS ward on the East Coast and one of the oldest HIV treatment programs in the country. Located in the West Village and near Chelsea, it was ground zero of the AIDS epidemic.

No hospital is welcoming. It's about negotiating the front desks, getting the visitor's pass, and finding my way to the room hoping that I would see nothing horrid or hideous or excessively painful on the way there. I managed it. No matter how designers may labor at making hospitals seem less foreboding, there are not enough cheerful paint colors or pleasantly neutral framed prints or comfortable plastic chairs to make them anything other than hospitals. The light is too intense, the smell of antiseptic too caustic, and the pain absorbed by the walls all too palpable for me. I braved it for Sam.

There he was in bed, fully conscious yet diminished as only a hospital gown can diminish someone. He seemed to have folded in on himself, to have shrunk. He must have known that he was dying. He frequently used to say that his father had died at age fifty-four and he knew that he wouldn't pass him in years. Here, though, Sam was frightened and had entered the hospital system in such a way that in the words of his best friend's book title, nobody knew his name. He had been admitted to the hospital as an indigent; no one knew just how he got there or in what state. It seems he was simply admitted as an unknown Black man without any identification about his status in life. They seemed to know little about him and nurses and interns alike were shocked at my telling them that Samuel Clemens Floyd III was a respected English professor at Queens College.

Sam, although apprehensive and in discomfort, was being his usual cantankerous self, and I tried to pour some oil on the troubled waters that his hair-trigger temper had already managed to roil. I also explained that not only was he a professor at one of the city colleges, he was also a close friend of Maya Angelou and James Baldwin. As a result of my father's multiple bouts of illness, I had more experience than I wanted with the functioning of hospitals and wanted to be sure that Sam had all of the care he deserved, so I pitched a very sedate hissy fit and let all know that this was not human detritus simply because he'd arrived without fanfare. This was an individual with family, professional status, and a world of friends (some of them world famous) who loved him very, very much.

In all of the scurrying and hurrying, I did notice that the nursing staff was being particularly careful with their handling of Sam. When I initially visited him, he was in a two-bedded room and there were no indicators that something very serious was wrong. There, small and diminished in the hospital bed, he remained the North Carolina gentleman until the end, covering himself with the thin blanket and using what strength he had left to play host, offer the occasional bon mot, and generally entertain as though seated in his high-backed chair a few blocks over on Horatio Street.

He recognized me and looked at me through half-closed eyes and seemed to relax back murmuring, "I knew you'd come; I knew you'd be here." He was parched with lips chapped from fever, and I swabbed his mouth out, got him some ice to suck on, sat with him for a while until it was evident that he was too tired for company, and then left, saying that I'd see him the following day.

I alerted the circle of friends. We didn't visit en masse. Rather, we each journeyed to the hospital to visit and be astonished into realizing how sick he had become. We each had our private and personal moments of good-bye. More than thirty years later, Louise Meriwether could still recall the look of bereft shock on David Baldwin's face as he stared at Sam through the closing doors of the isolation ward for one last time. No one had expected this. It wasn't happening.

In the words of the Dinah Washington that he so loved, what a difference a day makes. By my visit the next day, they'd obviously taken some tests and made some diagnoses. The nurses still gave no indication of what might have been wrong, but they were guarded as they were with all patients at this time. Sam had been put in isolation, a sign that they were not sure what he had. From the protocols that had been put into place, it was obvious that they thought he had AIDS. AIDS! How could that have happened! Less than a month prior, we'd been acting like old lovers and but for a nod and an unusual tug of restraint would have tumbled back into bed. AIDS? How could that be? Sam wasn't gay; we'd slept together, after all, and reveled in each other's bodies. He wasn't an IV drug user, he certainly wasn't Haitian, and he wasn't a hemophiliac. Gay?

Gay I knew. Jimmy was gay. Darrell was gay. Patrick was gay. Lowell was gay. Any number of my other friends and acquaintances were gay. Bisexuality . . . that I didn't understand. I took things and people at face value and as they told me and as they acted. Sam had been my lover; he'd been Maya Angelou's lover and friend and had boasted of his relationships with Diana Sands and others. I knew all of this, and in my naiveté there was no reason for me to think otherwise. There had been hints. A report that he'd been seen coming out of one of the notorious clubs and a look at the male friends with whom he'd surrounded himself. Baldwin had tried to alert me. At one gathering, he'd looked over at me and commented cryptically to my mother, "Tell your daughter that which I cannot tell her." My mother, the Baptist minister's daughter from New Jersey, had no idea what he was trying to say or what point he was trying to make. She dutifully reported the brief exchange to me. I'd actually been there and had heard him, but try as we could to parse it out, neither of us had any more of an idea what he was saying than the other, so we discussed it and then buried the thought. His was the only hint, the only warning alarm. What had happened? What had I missed? What markers had I ignored? It was a massive question mark. What had begun all those years ago after the meal at my friend's apartment in SoHo, lived itself out so joyfully with trips and complicity and genuine affection and, yes, love, ended badly with tears, questions, and confusion.

Sam died of AIDS on April 1, 1986, in what was clearly a cosmic April Fool's joke. Others took over, and I did what I had become very good at doing: I eclipsed myself and disappeared into my own world. Sam was cremated; few would embalm those with AIDS. In fact and indeed, Sam's funeral arrangements were not up to any one of the friends. Sam's next of kin were his sisters, who did appear and collect the ashes, and whatever life insurance and death benefits he had. Sam's mother was also alive when he died, and I like to believe that his ashes made their way home to his quietly sedate mother in North Carolina and found rest in the town that he loved so much.

• • •

Maya at one point had called to ask me how I was, and from her, I heard that there were some plans for the friends to have a memorial of some sort at some time. I demurred, chafing at being considered the "grieving widow" when Sam and I hadn't been a couple in quite some time. It was a toxic combination of grief and denial; I had stepped away to adjust to the lightning bolt strike of Sam's bisexuality and the fact that I seemed to be the only one in the crowd who didn't know. Other than Jimmy's mention to my mother, no one over the years had said a mumbling word. I withdrew; it was the only way that I knew to distance myself from Sam's death from AIDS, come to grips with my own feelings of insecurity about it all, and acknowledge just how closely the angel of death's dark wing had again passed to me. The two formative men in my life gone in less than a year: my father and now Sam, my spiritual "other."

The only memorial Sam had was a quiet one at Queens College in a small room in the Student Union. It was attended by a handful of colleagues, and it was the best that could be given by those who were mourning the loss of a colleague. A few words were read. Claiming the relationship that many at the school did not even know existed, I publicly read Maya's poem "To a Man"

My man is
Black Golden Amber

In the poem, Maya had revealed her deep love for Sam: his love of good brandy, his enveloping scent of Gitanes and Chanel Pour Homme, his southern manners, and his teasing, huggable plumpness. She had presented the man I had known, been intimate with, and loved with all of the passion that a twenty-something could muster. She'd also nailed him as ever changing. Indeed, he was like water: elusive, impossible to hold, and never to be contained. I now knew that.

Our Queens College colleague Corrine, who had been instrumental in organizing the memorial, spoke eloquently from her own grief about a man she had always loved but who could or would not reciprocate, and a small chamber music group of students and faculty played "Amazing Grace." It was sad not just because of the bereavement, the few attendees, and the program, but because it was an inappropriate finale for someone who had walked with the icons of music, literature, and the arts of the second half of the twentieth century and indeed been their equal. The informality, lack of style, and drab, unremarkable surroundings were totally inappropriate to Sam's life as he lived it.

From the circle of friends, there was nothing. There was a telephone call from Maya checking on the whereabouts of Sam's ashes and quietly asking if I was all right, but other than that nothing, only shock and astonishment that Sam was gone from a plague that had blindsided them all. At some point, Jimmy returned to town, and I saw him once,

but a year and a half later, in December 1987, he, too, would
be gone, memorialized in a service at St. John the Divine
that contained all of the pomp and majesty that he deserved:
African drumming and all of the pageantry of New York's
nonsectarian gothic cathedral underpinned by his mother's
mourning moans. I didn't know; I didn't go. Darrell died
earlier in 1987, and death had been too much with me. I
couldn't handle another memorial. I'd also disappeared
from the group. The fragile, tenuous bonds that I'd had with
them had dissolved at Sam's death, or so I thought.

Weeks after Sam's death, Corrine and Ruth, colleagues
from Queens College, obtained keys to Sam's apartment
from Lowell Todd with the hope of going by to begin to
clear it out. I was called to join them and did. The sorry
task was arduous. Sam, like me, was not a minimalist. It had
been years since I'd visited 81 Horatio Street, although I
still lived only a few blocks over, and the years had not been
kind. Blues, the cat, had preceded Sam in death by several
months, and left to his own devices with an illness that was
ravaging him, there had been no housekeeping. What had
been professorial disarray had turned into a cluttered pit
of stuff without the central illuminating soul that was Sam.
Books tumbled off shelves in the entrance, the bedroom,
and the living room. The ladder-back, cane-bottomed chair

still sat at the window, no longer a vantage point from which to view the world but, rather, a lonely memorial to what had been. In the kitchen, never pristine at the best of times, pots stood unwashed in the sink, coffee mugs awaited a good scrub, and the roaches were having their way. In the living room, the fireplace ashes were unhauled and papers overflowed from the coffee table from which Sam used to ceremoniously extract his latest pieces of writing. We read a few; this time, though, there were no compositions or snippets of character portraits or observations about life. They were revealing, painfully so, as though reading the diary of a longtime friend or parent in which deep secrets are told. There were instead letters to God and to an older church "sister" recalled from his youth, beseeching them to save him from whatever demons he felt were pursuing him and begging for relief. There were Fingerhut catalogues with strange, small items circled, nonessential trivial items of the sort he would have once derided as useless trash. The house had become a house of pain, isolation, and increasing dementia.

While we were doing this, Sam's sister Bernice called, cursing the colleagues out and telling them to leave everything and get out of her brother's apartment. I'd met Bernice and gone to visit her in her apartment in the Bronx a few times with Sam. He'd delighted in regaling folks with tales of his two sisters, who were his protectors and who were, in his telling of it, serious-drinking women who knew how to take care of themselves in the world—pistol-packing mamas for the twentieth century. Volatility clearly ran in the family, and Bernice also had the family hair-trigger temper. When they told her I was there with them, she was somewhat mollified, a testimonial to our kinder relationship and to her perceptions of my relationship with Sam. Nonetheless, we packed up what we were doing and left.

I had shared a good part of my youth with Sam and we'd lived in dual-apartment symbiosis with items shared back and forth between our conjoined households. I looked for none of the things that I had loaned him: the signed books, first editions, and galleys from my book-reviewing days were crated up and eventually went to Corrine. The cooking utensils that journeyed from one apartment to the other for dinner parties and suppers remained in the cabinets and on the shelves. I left the apartment with a few items, the scant detritus of a formative time that would never be repeated: a silver stuffing spoon, a carving knife, a Blue Willow turkey platter, two service plates (one from Chez Garin and the other from Le Lingousto), an unopened bottle of Chanel Pour Homme (the fragrance that I will forever connect with Sam), and one large black-and-white photograph of Sam with an unknown man standing by a motorcycle. I did not know the man, nor did Corrine or Ruth; he looked a bit like a blond biker type. Sam is smiling and looks sublimely happy and connected to him. I did not know the man, but

I did know the shirt that Sam was wearing: one of the batik ones that he had gotten from his Barbadian friend, Stella St. John. I kept the photo to remind me that things are not always as they seem and that face value may not always be all that there is. My Sam Floyd period had ended with revelations and confusion. The final coda, though, would not come until more than fourteen years later.

I can't cook now. I'll just drink.

While the crowd may have done their mourning with Johnnie (Walker), Jack (Daniel's), and Jim (Beam), I sustained myself with red wine and lots of it. I'd moved from the jug wines and reduced-for-sale-bin bottles into my Merlot moment and was developing a palate. Now I've gone beyond that into the occasional very good Burgundy and American Pinot Noir. So crack open the piggy bank and pour a Baccarat goblet full of Gevrey-Chambertin, Romanée-Conti, or some ruby velvet liquid from Willamette Valley to celebrate the full life that was Sam's.

Chapter Nine

AFTERMATH

After Sam's death, I'd dropped out, but the circle of friends and friendships continued. Feeling like a sexual pariah through no fault of my own, I remained firmly on the edge, leaving it all behind. Two years later, I bought a house in Brooklyn, left the West Village, and embarked on another part of my own life. It was over, or so I thought. It now seems logical that Dolly McPherson would have been the glue that held it all together for me.

A native of New Orleans, McPherson had, like Sam and the members of the group who erred on the academic side of the equation, grown up in the old-school world of HBCUs. When I met her, she was teaching at Hunter College. Not only was Dolly Maya's litmus test at Wake Forest, she would later become her Boswell as well, writing an analysis of her growing autobiographical oeuvre. Dolly was a true southern belle, always gracious and a bit formal, but she also had a wicked sense of humor and could hold her own with any of the crowd. Dolly also had a kindness and an openness with me that may have stemmed from the fact that Sam was a friend and not a former lover, and we became fast, if irregular, friends. I suspect, as she had with students over the years, Dolly was quietly mentoring me.

Like Sam, and indeed like me, Dolly was a spendthrift, and the joke ran that she would take the subway to Sam's apartment to borrow some money and then return home in a taxi once the transaction was completed. McPherson's apartment was appropriately professorial, filled with the bulging bookshelves that seemed to be a prerequisite for entrance into the group of friends.

Dolly was Maya's conscience in many ways: her kinder and gentler side. Dolly was one of the few people who could and would disagree with Maya and hold her own. It was a valuable role as Maya's fame increased and fewer and fewer people would disagree with her.

Dolly kept up with folks and knit her friendships closely; Dolly kept in touch. After Sam's death, Dolly stayed in touch with me and with my mother, gently supporting endeavors, savoring triumphs, marking book publications, and generally keeping up with news. It was logical, then, that she was the one I turned to when my mother died in 2000. It happened so suddenly that I found myself at sea. Although eighty-seven years old, my mother had been resistant to any thoughts of death, and so when she died, there were no plans for anything, only a very full house that we'd lived in for almost fifty years and a lifetime of happy memories. When my father had died fifteen years earlier, Mom and I had each other, but this time I was truly alone, and I had no idea where to turn. As I had no significantly older female relatives, I could only look to those elders whom I'd known with Sam. Dolly, who had been a friend to my mother and me, was one of my first calls.

Somehow I knew that Dolly's positive voice and elder sister wisdom was what I needed, so I called her, finding her number in one of my mother's telephone books. She answered and was the calm, nurturing soul that I needed. She suggested that I might want Maya to speak at Mom's memorial. I'd never considered that she might and certainly had not dared to think of asking for such a favor, but Dolly felt that she would and was more than willing to make the call. Shortly after, I heard the familiar voice on the phone comforting me and saying that she would come to New York to speak. I was floored but grateful and went about making the other plans and organizing a memorial. (We don't do funerals in my immediate family.)

As is often the case with bereavements, there were and

still are holes in my memory about those days, and my scattershot organizing of things meant that there were also many changes of plan. As an only child, this one was completely on me, and I had no idea where to begin. I can only claim that I was guided from beyond, because a voice reminded me of my mother's family's undertaker, who agreed to take on all of the arrangements for cremation and the sad tasks of getting the death certificate and other requisites. My parents had been charter members of the church I grew up in, and I'd in fact been the first baby christened in the congregation, so the venue was taken care of. Slowly, it all came together. Friends flocked from around the world, and somehow arrangements for the memorial service, a repast, and all of the other things from program printing to lodgings for out-of-town guests were taken care of. I still don't know how, but will always be grateful to all of my friends who surrounded me then. It all went off without a hitch, until in the middle of the repast following the memorial that had to change the original date because the church had a prior commitment, the phone rang and someone said, "Jessica, it's for you; it's someone who says she's Maya Angelou." I'd completely forgotten my request and had never felt that she would have made such a trek from North Carolina for me. Mortified, I went to the phone, my embarrassment trumping my grief, and explained my horror at my mistake and my not informing her of the date change.

There was quiet; then that calm and soothing voice said, "I understand." In truth, a part of me hadn't believed that she would travel to New York for me! For me!

The next day, I journeyed to where she was staying in Manhattan to beg pardon and take the licks that I certainly deserved. There were none. I don't remember where we met; I do remember overflowing bookcases and comfortable chairs and sitting at Maya's feet and giving her the unfinished caged bird cloisonné pendant that my mother had begun for Dolly but had not been able to finish. I remember little else from that meeting but the caring familial warmth with which I was enveloped.

It was the beginning of a new chapter between Maya and me, one where Sam remained the unmentioned glue that united us, but where we met as, if not equals (I was still very much the younger sister), then adults: adults who had weathered some storms together and shared memories of a past that few others knew.

I gradually came back into the now-expanded fold. Jimmy was no longer the sun at the center of this circle of friends; rather, Maya had become the reigning monarch. She had bought a Harlem brownstone that soon became the hub of her New York universe. Gloriously renovated, as can happen when funds are seemingly endless, it was designed for entertaining, with bold colors and comfortable seating. One could enter either from the basement kitchen level or climb the brownstone's steps and be received more formally at the front door. It was clearly divided into public spaces and private ones, and there was little crossing of them. An elevator had been installed so that Maya could slip in and out of the room without climbing the steps, which had become increasingly difficult for her to navigate with age.

The public spaces consisted of the living room, where Maya is reputed to have asked the decorator to give her a fruit bowl. The strawberry, watermelon, and banana colors were vivid and welcoming and very much like falling into a vibrant fruit bowl. This was a public room—one for grand pronouncements and posed photographs, for holiday festivities and bold-faced moments.

The dining area was a bit more sober. Decorative painting of a cloud-filled brilliant-blue sky made the ceiling a cry thrown up to heaven. Crimson chairs surrounded a circular dining table at which all were on equal footing, as though we were in King Arthur's court at the Round Table. At her festivities, the elders from the circle that I had known convened when they were in attendance. Rosa, who was beginning to show signs of the Alzheimer's that would eventually afflict her, Louise Meriwether, and Joan Sandler camped out in the cushy chairs surrounding the dining room. It was here that Maya often sat, and here that she said grace before we ate, beginning with her usual invocation, "Mother, Father,

God . . ." One New Year's Day, the conversation and the energy around that table were so vital and vibrant that the glass that topped the table cracked right down the middle. All stopped for a minute. Then the ancestors were saluted and acknowledged and everything went on as before, making allowances, of course, for the glass with a big crack down the middle.

The basement kitchen/sitting room was a more intimate space where the plush cushions were dented with butt prints from intimate conversations, and there was a cozy comfort that signaled home and hearth, not house beautiful. It was a sort of neutral ground between the public space of the upstairs reception rooms and the very private bedroom spaces above where few others than family ventured. The kitchen was designed with an island that could serve as a buffet serving space for large gatherings. It did double duty as delineator of space when Maya cooked, and looking at it the first time, I vividly recalled the culinary performance so many years before in Sonoma. Now, though, when I was in the kitchen, I was no longer simply a spectator; we'd cook together, bonding for real this time over our shared passion for food and our common love for entertaining. Maya loved people, reveled in good company, and adored entertaining. She gave parties: small dinners and lavish y'all-come gatherings to which all of her known world was invited. These parties had gone on all along in other venues and at other times, but after my return to the group, I became aware of them through Maya's New Year's Day party.

The party was a New York humdinger of a gathering. I began attending it annually, returning from New Orleans, where I'd begun to spend the Christmas holidays and the end-of-the-year festivities. All ages mixed and mingled at the New Year's Day gatherings: family, friends old and new, business associates, and acquaintances who seemed to be interesting. Ironically, I too had thrown New Year's Day parties and had hosted as many as sixty people in my home in Brooklyn; they were similar in many other ways as well, reminding me just how I'd been formed by that circle of friends more than thirty years earlier. Mine, though, were small things compared to Maya's, which were huge, splendid, and helmed by her more-than-able personal assistant, Lydia Stuckey, to whom I took an immediate liking. Maya did all of the cooking for the New Year's Day parties, reveling in the chance to show off her culinary skills and delighting in creating a lavish spread of all of the traditional foods that make up New Year's Day in an African American household. There were black-eyed peas and rice (served separately, not together) and made with and without pork, greens, potato salad, macaroni and cheese, sweet potatoes, and several types of turkey, along with roast ham—all prepared in what a West African girlfriend of mine would have called "industrial quantities." This lavish spread was accompanied by rivers of red wine and scotch and a bounty of desserts. After dinner, there was often caroling with professional voices singing traditional songs while Valerie Simpson accompanied folks on the piano. Presents were exchanged with intimates, and I knew that Maya and I had passed another milestone on the friendship trail when one year she made sure that I received a small something, a token of our enduring connection. I treasure my Indian pillboxes.

I found myself one of the crowd and saw folks I'd known from my early years of theater reviewing and career as a fledgling journalist. George Faison and his partner, T, were regulars. George was a dancer extraordinaire who years ago had choreographed *The Wiz* and garnered awards including a Tony and an Emmy, before becoming an impresario at the Faison Firehouse Theatre in Harlem. Marcia Gillespie had been editor in chief of *Essence* when I began there and then moved on to helm *Ms.* magazine and continue to influence a generation. Howard Dodson, with his ever-present cowrie shell pin decorating his lapel, was head of the Schomburg Center and another regular. Most important, there were Louise Meriwether and Rosa Guy and Helen Brodie Baldwin, Jimmy's sister-in-law and Lover's widow. It was like old home week the first time I went and refound acquaintances I hadn't seen since my Sam Floyd years. There were new faces as well: Nick Ashford and Valerie Simpson, whose music had been the background music for much of my youth, were stalwarts and among Maya's adopted extended family, as were numerous other notables. I found that I savored the jaunts; they became my way of beginning the year Janus-like, looking backward to look forward.

Over time, I got comfortable enough (or consumed enough red wine) to compare rings with Nick Ashford, who admired my antique black cameo collection. I shared the name of my antique jewelry dealer; he could afford the habit more than I. I brought guests with permission, sharing my very famous friend with some of my other friends and letting her know how my life had expanded. Haroldo and Mary Costa from Brazil attended one year, and Haroldo, who had been the original Orfeu in the play that would go on to become the film *Orfeu and Eurydice*, was so impressed with Maya that he still speaks of it years later. At one party, I was bold enough to sit on the piano bench alongside Valerie Simpson and caterwaul a few of what I hoped were on-key notes. I enjoyed the time I spent at the house on 120th Street.

On occasion, it seemed that nothing had changed and as though Jimmy might be around the corner in another room enveloped in a cloud of cigarette smoke, his hands flutter-ing like hummingbirds while he explained the ways of the world to some young votary, or Sam might dance in waving a beaker of Johnnie Walker and wafting a cloud of Chanel Pour Homme. But the crowd had changed and the focus had shifted. Angelou was now firmly the center of the orbit. Paule had moved on, but Louise and Rosa were still there (until 2012 when Rosa died). At times it almost seemed that despite Maya's worldwide fame and considerably increased fortune, little had changed in the pecking order. We had all aged, but we had all aged in sequence; I remained twenty years younger than Maya and younger than Louise, Rosa, and Paule by exactly the same distance that had existed in the 1970s. I was still the kid, the youngest of that bunch despite my gray hair and widening waist.

After our initial reconnection and my attendance at the New Year's Day festivities, other offers of hospitality were proffered. There was one Super Bowl party Maya gave where she had purchased souvenir jerseys of the teams for her guests and we sat around discussing everything but football. The television was playing downstairs, in another part of the house, but most folks could have cared less about the game.

I especially enjoyed going in the evenings when there was no one else there so that I basically spent time with Maya and Ms. Stuckey, whom Maya unfailingly introduced as Ms. Stuckey with her insistence on formality. She's always made a point of presenting people and especially anyone who might be conceived of as being in a subordinate position—housekeepers, cooks, companions, secretaries, drivers, and others—as Mr., Mrs., or Ms. I suspected that it was more than southern formality. It was a very real reaction to having grown up in the South and watched so many of her elders being called "out of their names" and disrespectfully by their first names for so many years. Through that, I also understood just why she insisted on being called Dr. Angelou and why she bridled when people she did not know well called her Maya. The honorific was always required and *always* used even by her closest friends. I, somehow, called her Maya, and I believe I was allowed to do so in acknowledgment of when I had entered her life those four decades prior, when she was still just Maya.

On our solo evenings, we talked about all manner of things. I savored the company, our developing closeness, and the connection to the past and began to visit when she was in town and share thoughts with her. We were still guarded and tentative with a respect for each other's feelings. There remained something unspoken between us—a fragile thread that was our different links to Sam and our unspoken and yet shared knowledge of things that had transpired all those decades prior.

In truth, Maya was still Maya, and I was still stubborn.

On one of our evenings, Maya discovered my continuing grief over my mother's death. I retained Mom's voice on my answering machine at my office; I'd discovered the message after her death. I'd call in every two weeks from wherever I was (often at great expense if I was in West Africa or the Caribbean) just to hear her voice and her sign-off of the conversation, "God be with you!" Deciding that it was excessive and wanting to help me through the grief, Maya offered to stay with me while I deleted the message. I demurred and kept it, allowing it to fade organically from my life several years later.

Another evening she surprised me by saying out of the blue, "You know, Jessica, it is all right to have loved a gay man!" Gay man? Sam? You, my elder sister, knew and you didn't tell me? You didn't shepherd me through the danger-water time that occurred after he died from AIDS? There were too many dragons in that closet to even think of opening the door, and that conversation never continued, changing rapidly to some banal subject that was safer ground for us both. I always wonder what the outcome would have been if we'd been brave enough to have had a longer conversation. Confession? Apology? Commiseration? We did cross a line that evening, one that brought us closer despite the lack of intimate conversation.

On occasion Maya would reach out to me, calling to ask for a recipe (ginger beer was one special request). We even did one of her Sirius radio shows together and spent an hour gleefully sharing our love of food and cooking like two best friends talking over a back fence. We shared a love for New Orleans, but she visited infrequently because of her allergy to fish, which kept her in fear of the restaurants in the city, where virtually everything is prepared with crabmeat, crawfish, or shrimp. As one who is allergic to shellfish, I could sympathize and empathize and became deputized to find some places where she would be able to sample the other side of the city's food. When we both happened to be in New Orleans at the same time—she'd always let me know when she was going to be in town—I'd try to be there and she'd call. Often it was with a small request like asking me to search for a book of her poems that she wished to read from or join her for dinner or recommend a restaurant where she might be able to get a meal that was not cooked near seafood. It was her way of staying in touch.

It was in New Orleans after a meal that she told me in confidence about the aches and pains of her dancer's knees. They plagued her but were inoperable because of a lung condition that meant it was unwise for her to consider anesthesia. This was confided on a walk to the ladies' room at a hotel in New Orleans prior to a lecture she'd be giving. At a later point, again in New Orleans, she let me know she'd be heading out immediately after the lecture because her lung issue had become so difficult, she could not be without her oxygen machine for more than one hour. Her lectures were timed to the nanosecond. Following her last word, despite lavish applause and standing ovations, she would be escorted off the stage and immediately return to her breathing apparatus. Hindsight lets me know that she was increasingly allowing me into her confidence and reattaching me to her and through her to that circle of friends.

On the last trip to New Orleans where I joined her, she arrived in town in splendor, riding on the bus that Oprah had given her. It made things much easier, and the lavish accommodations were as comfortable as any hotel could have possibly been. She graciously allowed me to bring a guest, this time Danille Taylor, then dean of humanities at Dillard University, where I was the inaugural scholar in the Ray Charles Chair in African American Material Culture (a position that I knew Sam, with his love of HBCUs, would have been proud to see me accept). We shared drinks and marveled at the bus's comfort: bathtub, bedrooms, sleeping area for two drivers so that they could spell each other and never have to stop. It was a setting fit for the empress of popular literature that she'd become. I brought along cheese straws prepared for her by a friend's daughter in fish-free surroundings, and we shared our usual conviviality.

Along with New Year's festivities in New York, Maya also

gave a magnificent Thanksgiving celebration in Winston-Salem, where her main house was located. There, she'd entertain as many as two hundred people at dinner, pulling out all of the stops and creating an event that turned into a weekend extravaganza, complete with organized manicures and facials for the women, church services on Sunday for all attendees, and, of course, a lavish Thanksgiving dinner for all. Although I was invited on several occasions, tangential seemed to be the best place for me. I do not like hordes of people, and my relationship with Maya seemed to flourish best on a one-on-one basis. I'd been invited to Winston-Salem at other times of the year, but I'd always demurred, knowing that there was still unspoken conversation between us and things that needed straightening out. Finally, I also knew that Maya still drank with the same quiet, ferocious determination that marked everything she did, and I didn't want to be caught alone in the house with her if the liquor started to speak. So I continued to go to the New Year's Day parties, becoming a bit of a regular. I even met Guy, Maya's son; I'd not met him during the Sam Floyd years.

One year though, I'd arrived and timidly headed to my usual spot in the dining room on the perimeter of the round table where I could be near Maya and also Louise and Rosa. Guy, who was there as well and did not know me, was getting ready to say something about my presence at the table, when quietly, with her usual control and grace, Maya told him that I in fact did belong at the table. She informed him how long I'd known her and insisted that I join the crowd of elders at her large circular table, the focal point of her festivities. There, looking around at Rosa, Louise, and Maya and thinking of the years we'd known one another and the roads that had been taken, I marveled at the distance that we'd traveled separately together.

Gradually I came to feel myself to be a regular in Maya's circle, but my illusions of being a real part of the crowd were squelched one year. Having journeyed from New Orleans in time to make what had become the annual party. Intuition kicked in, and I thought, or as Maya would have put it, "my Toby hunched me," that before embarking on the fifty-dollar taxi ride that would take me to Harlem, I'd better call, as I'd heard from no one. I called and got no answer. Well, that just might mean that the house was full and no one heard the phone, but after three or four calls, I realized that something was up. I searched my phone and realized that I had George Faison's number and called him. I was gob-smacked when he said they were not in Harlem at all but had decided that year to go to Florida and were basking beside the pool in Miami.

I spent that New Year's Day by myself in New York and made my black-eyed peas, collards, and pork dinner from the just-in-case set of leftovers that I keep in my freezer. (I'd rather have stale frozen leftovers than challenge the gods by not having my Hoppin' John, greens, and pig on New Year's Day.) After that, I extended my New Orleans stay to include festivities with friends in that town and said good-bye to the New Year's Day parties. It was now over for sure, or so I thought.

Maya Angelou's New Year's Kale

Greens are traditional on African American New Year's tables. If Hoppin' John means luck, the greens are for folding money. The type of greens is not specified and different families have their own traditions. My family went with collards, so that's what I crave on January first. In her cookbook Hallelujah! The Welcome Table, *Maya Angelou gave us her recipe for collard greens. It uses turkey wings. However, according to her personal assistant of many years, Lydia Stuckey, she preferred the taste of kale and usually served kale at her expansive table on New Year's Day—and she prepared it with a ham hock. It was not your healthy kale that is currently of the moment, but a down-home rendition of a holiday classic. The non-swine-eating folks didn't mind in the least; there were so many other dishes in her lavish spread and plenty of delights for them to savor.*

– Serves four –

1 meaty ham hock
4 pounds fresh kale, picked over
 and cleaned, with the tough
 center stem removed
2 medium onions, finely chopped
¼ teaspoon minced hot red
 chiles, or to taste

Salt and freshly ground black
 pepper, to taste
Hot sauce, to taste
Vinegar, to taste

Place the ham hock in water to cover, bring to a boil, then lower the heat and simmer for 1½ hours. Add the kale, half of the chopped onions, the chiles, salt, pepper, and more water, if needed and continue to cook until the ham hock is falling off the bone and the greens are done. Serve with the hot sauce, vinegar, and the remaining chopped onions.

Chapter Ten

IT AIN'T OVER 'TIL IT'S OVER!

But even that was not the end of things. I had learned from Sam and Jimmy that "every good-bye ain't gone and every shut eye ain't sleep." The saying is correct. It ain't over until it's over, and my time with Maya and the folks who remained in the circle of friends was not over as I thought it was.

After I stopped seeing Maya in Harlem, I was invited to keynote a conference at the University of North Carolina in Greensboro in February 2014 and accepted gladly. Although I'm pretty good on distances and locations of most of the major cities in Europe, West Africa, and the Caribbean, I'm more than a bit geographically challenged about locations in the United States. I was surprised, glancing in the airplane magazine on the flight down, to notice that Greensboro was not that far from Winston-Salem, where Maya had her primary residence. After a quick calculation with MapQuest, I realized that Winston-Salem was not really distant. It was the first time I'd spent a length of time in North Carolina, and I felt guilty at the prospect of being in the state and not trying to see Maya. The knowledge that we were proximate and, who knows, perhaps the sense that time was fading and that we needed to see each other made me pick up the phone. I called and, as she unfailingly did, she came to the phone and seemed delighted when I told her that I was in the vicinity and asked if I could visit. She sent Mr. Stanback, her driver, to pick me up at the hotel and bring me to her house. (To this day, I get into taxis in New York City and greet the astonished drivers with a good morning, afternoon, or evening before announcing where I'm headed. I used to add their name, Mr. So-and-So, before the print on the Taxi and Limousine Commission licenses got too small to read. It's a lasting part of my training from Maya back in the day.)

Mr. Stanback negotiated the roads with studied skill, and in a little over an hour, we pulled through the gates of her home. This was home on another level—one where there were palpably deeper roots than in New York, with a softer, calmer color palette. House proud, Maya introduced me to her helpers and asked one of them to give me a tour, and I marveled at it all. Near the living room was the throne-like writing room. It was almost Shaker-like in its austerity, and dead center in the room, a high-backed, straight-backed chair sat at a small desk surrounded by four walls filled with books. There was little of the clutter and detritus of my own working environment, but rather a space that spoke of the iron discipline and steel will that got Maya there. The basement was a rabbit warren of rooms, each filled to overflowing with bookshelves on every available wall space that wasn't filled with visually stunning art. Her pride was the home's formal dining room and the enormous outdoor entertainment area in which she joyously hosted a growing tribe of relatives and friends with frequency.

When I returned from the tour—glorious dining room, expansive living room, guest rooms, entertaining spaces, and an open kitchen like the one that I recalled from so many years ago in Sonoma—she was sitting at the head of the kitchen table, a stack of clipped *New York Times* crossword puzzles at her right hand with pen at the ready, a small pile of the books she was reading and a yellow pad of paper at her left, and a glass of scotch within reach. Although tethered to the oxygen machine that by then had been her constant for years, she was very much Maya: imperious and imperial—the phenomenal woman at home. I'd finally made it to Winston-Salem.

Increasingly over the years, we had bonded over our love of good food, good cooking, and the culture that is carried in it. I was therefore in no way surprised when in 2004 she wrote her first cookbook, and it mixed recipe and recount-

ing. In print, it re-created the astonishing culinary performance I'd witnessed in Sonoma decades earlier. Knowing
this, I'd taken her a signed copy of my friend Maricel Pre-
silla's award-winning cookbook, *Gran Cocina Latina*; she was
delighted and not only intrigued by the dishes and their history, but looking forward to cooking from the book. She
cooked recipes from all over the world—not only items
from her vast collection of cookbooks but her own dishes
created from loving the way that two ingredients combined,
the way a spice set off a meat or vegetable, or simply the
coordinated colors that they formed on the plate.

A gourmet without being a gourmand, she became conscious of weight in later years. I will always remember her
advice on dieting: "I take a bite or two of something. Then I
say to myself, 'Now I know what that tastes like, I don't have
to devour it all.'" It's excellent advice but requires amazing
self-discipline, which she had in spades. Until the end, she
retained a questing curiosity about culinary cultures. She'd
traveled the world and retained many of its flavors in her taste
buds. She especially excelled at traditional African American
foods, the slow-cooked country foods of her youth; they
were not just the soul-nourishing fare that she loved but also
stood for tradition, history, and connectedness.

We cooked together again, and I had a flashback to the
virtuosic dinner demonstration of more than forty years
prior. Maya, although this time anchored by her breath-

ing apparatus, was still in charge. She kept cooked chickens in the freezer where they could be thawed at will and then quickly stripped off the bone and transformed into chicken salad and other dishes that she enjoyed. That day, she felt like chicken salad. Small bowls appeared as the mise en place for the salad—chicken stripped from the carcass, minced celery, a bit of minced onion, mayonnaise, salt and pepper. She mixed, tested, and tasted, verifying flavor and consistency. It was missing something—mustard, she decided. Ordinary American ballpark mustard was produced, added, a final taste, and it was pronounced ready. It was perfection; we ate it for lunch.

We both seemed to sense that this might be the last time we saw each other, that our time together was drawing to a close. And as I left, elated to have reconnected and wanting not to lose the fragile thread that we'd reknit from memories and food, I asked if I could come back the next day. "Of course," she said graciously, and I made my arrangements with Mr. Stanback for transportation.

For Black women, perhaps the most intimate test for friendship is letting another watch as you have your hair done. There's an incremental intimacy that goes from watching you have your hair washed to sitting between a friend's legs and having it braided. There is a special intimacy and a vulnerability that comes with watching someone having her hair straightened. For those of us of a certain age, it is a journey in five senses: the heat of the hot comb, the slight sizzle it makes on the hair oil as it "fries" the hair straight, the smell of heat and oil, the vulnerability that comes from having tender scalp near heated metal comb, and finally the understanding that this is a very personal moment, a glimpse into another level of reality. Finally, for many of us, it's a time-traveling trip back to childhood, complete with its own vocabulary with words like *tender headed* and *kitchen*, and *nappy* and *kinky*.

The last visit that I had with Maya was on that level of intimacy. Her hairdresser had come by to prepare her for an appearance that she was making via satellite television. She was too exhausted to make the appearance person- ally, and teams had been sent to set up cameras and lights so that she could speak from her home. She was having her hair done in preparation. Talking with her as the hair- dresser tended to her duties, we took our friendship to a deeper level, and I could even imagine having a glimpse of the Maya she must have been as a child getting her hair done to appear in some church pageant in Stamps, Arkan- sas, like the one she detailed so vividly in *I Know Why the Caged Bird Sings*.

We shared another meal, this time a hot dog—one of the simple foods that she loved. The same care went into its preparation that had gone into making the chicken salad a day earlier. Condiments called for and assembled, bun toasted, and dog cooked just so. She ate with diminished appetite and only wanted half, but the small amount that she consumed, she ate with gusto. It would be our last meal together. After the years of takeout orders from El Faro, lavish suppers cooked by Sam, Paparazzi pasta dinners, and the meals she'd cooked, including the astonishing one in Sonoma more than forty years prior, it's ironic indeed that our last meal together would be a simple hot dog lunch eaten off a kitchen table crowded with the detritus of everyday living.

A close friend dropped by after the hairdresser left, and scotch was called for. Our time for intimate conversation had passed with too much left unsaid. With the friend's arrival, the conversation changed slightly. We talked about parents (he'd recently lost his mother) and legacy and life and its twisting turns. Another libation was called for, and the friend and I were sent off to get liquor from the shed that served as a depot. We went off chatting companionably (perhaps a bit too much so). When we returned, I could tell that things had changed, and it was time for me to go. When I suggested it might be time for me to leave, it was confirmed with a "Yes, it's time for you to go." I left with Mr. Stanback and headed back to my hotel; that was the last time I saw Maya.

• • •

Thomas Stearns Eliot lied. April is *not* the cruelest month. It's May. The not-so-merry month of May. May marks the month in which both of my parents died fifteen years and thirteen days apart and it's also the month in which Maya died fourteen years after my mother. Ironically, I was in New Orleans when I received word of Maya's death. An early-rising friend of mine, not knowing that I was in another time zone, awakened me at 5:00 a.m. with the sad news. Then there was no more sleep, only memories flowing in an endless loop: Sam and Jimmy and Horatio Street, and Dolly and Rosa and Paule and Louise, and bourbon and ginger ale and takeout from El Faro, and dancing to Stevie Wonder in platform shoes, and my own parents, and my youth, and the journey shared and the friendships savored and the better part of my life lived and past.

When death passes, arrangements have to be initiated and calls were made to Winston-Salem to determine what would happen. They'd not yet been made and were in the hands of Maya's immediate and extended family. I said a quiet, personal good-bye to my longtime friend in my sun-dappled garden and awaited the news. When the announcements came, I was appalled to note that I had an inviolable commitment on June 4, the day of the Winston-Salem memorial: I would be keynoting a conference on food that I'd organized in New Orleans. It was impossible to get out of that. When I called and attempted to explain my predicament, knowing full well just how tangential to everything I would be, I was told that there would be several memorials: one in San Francisco for the West Coast people and one in New York City at some unknown date later in the year. I began the New Orleans conference with a moment of silence in her memory and waited for the New York memorial.

The notice came during the summer that it would be held in the fall at Riverside Church in Manhattan. The invitation arrived, and I mused on the irony of a funeral invitation with an RSVP attached, but I did respond and requested not only my seat but my offered plus-one seat for a young protégée whom I'd asked to attend with me, knowing that she would be a way to connect future generations to that circle of friends. I duly received two tickets, which I put away, noting that the tag on the end said "silver," but thinking no more of it. I was surprised several weeks later to receive an email telling me that there had been a change in the seating arrangements and that I would receive a different ticket. Several weeks later I did, this one sporting a side tag that read "platinum." I'd been upgraded by someone. Again as she had at her own round table, Maya had reached out and moved me up, insisting that I own up to being a part of that circle of friends.

Riverside Church is New York's Notre Dame and Westminster Abbey all rolled up into one. While St. John the Divine may lay claim to being the city's handmade gothic masterpiece and St. Patrick's is where the pomp-and-circumstance funerals of Roman Catholic notables take place, Riverside Church is the people's church. It reflects the diversity of its neighborhood in every service and ceremony—a place imbued with the gravitas of organized religion. I'd been there a few times with a friend for services and savored the pluralistic service and the unique mix of smells and bells and happy/clappy rejoicing that could exist only in that New York City neighborhood. It was only fitting that it should be at Riverside Church that New York bid farewell to the woman who exemplified the spirit of a generation.

It was very much a celebrity memorial. There is no need to describe the service. In this era of oversharing, it was live-streamed, archived, and lives online where all can watch in their pajamas from home. Being there was another matter, another way of understanding and saying farewell. Folks were meeting and greeting, gossiping, looking for friends, and generally acting as though they were at a cocktail party and not a memorial. The to-ing and fro-ing and pew-hopping conversations before the ceremony began rivaled any at the latest nightclub, but the grief was real, as was the knowledge that we were all there bearing witness to the end of something powerful. My newly arranged platinum ticket placed me in the front pews with, surprisingly, friends and acquaintances I hadn't seen in decades. It was like being back at the New Year's party, only this time the gathering was a mix of the joy at reconnection muted by the somber solemnity of the occasion. Almost four months had passed since Maya's passing, so we'd all gotten over the shock, and watching the crowd at the pre-ceremony was enlightening. It was like watching a parade of my past life: Marcia Gillespie and Susan Taylor represented the *Essence* magazine years; Georges Faison, accompanied by his partner, T, was a nod to my theater-reviewing time; Helen Brodie Baldwin and Louise Meriwether took me back to my days with the circle of friends; and Toni Fay reminded me of my West Village days. There were others as well: some known, others familiar faces that had passed in corridors. The sanctuary was full; it was a standing-room-only crowd. The numbers of the stalwart, though, were diminishing: Rosa was gone; Joan Sandler, who could not make it, was represented by her daughter; I didn't see Paule. Luminaries, the kind who would appear in boldface in the *Post*, dotted the attendees. Space was being held in the front pews for Hillary Clinton and Valerie Simpson, and space had been left for the wheelchairs of Toni Morrison and Maya's son, Guy, all of whom would have a part in the services.

I was fascinated to see Toni. I'd seen little of her after the St. Paul sojourn, an occasional sighting as she ascended into the literary firmament that she now inhabits. I was pained to see that she arrived in a wheelchair, but the verve and the passion with which she spoke about her friend indicated that none of the fire had gone out.

The service was majestic, a fitting memorial for one who had become a cherished elder to the country and indeed the world. Hillary Clinton spoke. Songs were sung and chanted, and drums were beaten. Valerie Simpson performed a particularly moving mix of "I'm Every Woman" that included Maya's own voice and a coda sung to Morrison. I was astonished at the memorial to hear Guy say that he'd been terrified of her intensity most of his life, because I suspect I had been as well, as I had often been of Sam. They indeed were two of a kind. Their hair-trigger volatility made it hard for me·to figure them out and harder to see that in deed and in fact, they both truly loved me as much and as best as they knew how.

The repast that followed for the immediate family and friends was held at the Sugar Bar, the West Side venue owned by prime members of Maya's extended family: Nick Ashford and Valerie Simpson. Ashford himself had died three years prior, and a very visibly grieving and moved Simpson had not only sung at the service but, following that emotionally exhausting performance, she'd hosted the repast.

Not invited, still tangential to the group, I'd piggybacked attendance, relying on the company of Helen Brodie Baldwin, Jimmy's sister-in-law, and Louise Meriwether. With them, I edged into the table of elders who had known Maya for decades. There was Toni. Her aura of wisdom was palpable, and her face was familiar from so many book jackets and lecture posters, but it was undeniable that decades had passed and we had all grown older. Morrison, who had been in a wheelchair during the service, had difficulty walking, and her progress through the narrow restaurant was halting and painful. Helen was her usual voluble self, and she and Meriwether engaged in a friendly contest to snag the waiter to get some of the food that was clearly inadequate to serve the masses who'd shown up (including the uninvited like me). Word spreads rapidly about events like this, and without a doorman or a bouncer, they are easily overrun. Who would think there would be need for a gatekeeper at a repast following a memorial? Maya's certainly did.

Channeling my mother, I made myself known to Toni, who had no recollection of me. It was neither the time nor the place to struggle for markers that would have made me known. She was gracious and slightly apologetic at not remembering me, and asked one question: "Was I kind?" There were no words with which to describe just how kind she'd been. And how much the brief time that I did spend with her had meant and how it had formed me. The fact that that was her one question contains in itself a universe of information about the time and place that had been. Clearly I'd been a minute footnote in her very busy life, a tiny point that would take more digging than needed to be done, but the recognition of the possibility and the desire to have done no harm were telling of the kindnesses that she had indeed evidenced. For me, in the midst of the crowd, it was truly a time for reflecting about the past and about all that had been and those things left unsaid and so much that couldn't be said.

Divorced, beheaded, died. Divorced, beheaded, survived. So I was taught to remember the fate of the wives of Henry the Eighth. The fates have been only marginally kinder to the members of the group:

Richard Long, he of magisterial wisdom and astonishing linguistic abilities, died in 2013.

I have no idea what happened to Bernard Hassell, who danced at the Folies Bergère and guarded Jimmy's gates in St. Paul-de-Vence.

Benny Luke, who strutted his stuff in *La Cage aux Folles*, remained in Paris as a pillar of the African American community there. He died in 2013.

Georges Garin died in 1979 and was celebrated as a chef who pioneered nouvelle cuisine.

Mary Painter remained in the South of France, where she died in 1991.

Dolly McPherson was one of the few who could argue with Maya and reconnected me to the circle of friends. She remained Maya's sister/friend until forgetfulness slipped into the penumbra of Alzheimer's. She died in 2011.

Rosa Guy, Trinidadian author who transformed the world of young-adult literature with her frank presentations of the real-life issues that confront teenagers today, died in 2012.

Vertamae Smart-Grosvenor died in 2016, as I was finishing this book.

I have lost touch with Lowell Todd and do not know if he's still with us. He has moved from his Horatio Street apartment.

I have lost touch with Paule Marshall, but she lives and works in Virginia.

Corrine Jennings is the founding director and moving force behind Kenkeleba House, an art gallery on the Lower East Side. She has all of Sam's papers and books that we packed up over thirty years ago and hopes to one day use them as the foundation for an archive.

Louise Meriwether, who came to the parties with her mother and who was a pillar in the circle, is still very much alive and still very much writing.

Helen Brodie Baldwin, Lover's widow, lives in New

York City and attends all ceremonies honoring her late brother-in-law. She's writing her own story of life with the Baldwin family. We have meals together periodically.

Martina Arroyo no longer sings, but nurtures new talent through her Martina Arroyo Foundation. We are in touch after a many-year hiatus.

As I was beginning to research this book, I typed in a random collection of words—James Baldwin/Sam Floyd/France—and was astonished to find a posting about Baldwin from a man who stated that he knew Jimmy because he'd had a seventeen-year relationship with Professor Sam Floyd. Clearly that time overlapped with my Sam Floyd years in some way. I've tried to relocate the reference, but no matter what I type in, nothing comes up. The Internet gods have spoken, and I feel no need to open Pandora's box or pick at a healed-over wound. I've questioned those who knew, and whether from forgetfulness that comes with time or out of kindness for my youthful naiveté, they can recall no one else with Sam at my time. Whoever he is, I know he must have his own stories to tell, some of which no doubt parallel my own. Perhaps we'll meet; I suspect not. I loved Sam with all of the passion my twenty-year-old self could muster. Mercurial, majestic, maddening, and an eternal conundrum, Samuel Clemens Floyd III and the world to which he introduced me and the long-lasting friendships that I made because of him are a part of my DNA and I am me because of it.

As for Maya, a year or so after her passing, I attended a nonrelated event where I was surprised by Oprah's chef, Art Smith, when he looked up at me and said out of the blue, "Maya truly loved you, you know." Me? Really? No, I didn't know. The same scenario was repeated only last year by someone from Oprah's Sirius radio staff. With the hindsight that comes from close examination and with the wisdom (or at least experience) that comes with age, I can see that, yes, she did. We had a more-than-forty-year relationship that went from wariness to acceptance to affection and understanding. When I wrote *High on the Hog* in 2011, she, without question or quibble, wrote the Foreword, in which she extols my writing skills and presages this book by saying:

> If Harris decides that she is more of a prose writer than a recipe writer, the world of cookbook users and readers will be poorer for it. However, because she writes so well, all readers will be well serviced.
>
> I will be among that group.

I'm not sure how she would have felt about this effort. After all, no one more than she knew what it was to love

Sam Floyd, to be a part of that circle of friends, to have lived those times, and to have been a part of New York City at that very special moment in time. I like to think that, as with all of my other endeavors, she would have supported me as my soul looks back.

Leg of Lamb with Spicy Mint Sauce

I do much of my entertaining these days in the house that my parents bought more than fifty years ago on Martha's Vineyard. Both the island and I have changed a great deal in those years, but the gingerbread cottage overlooking the tennis courts will always be family home to me: a place that houses memories of people loved, friends made, and great meals shared. Many of the friends still summer on the Vineyard, and I celebrate the beginning of each new holiday with a shared Bastille Day meal that has leg of lamb as its centerpiece. It's my salute to memories of the past and friends of the present, and I try each year to include someone new as a look toward the future.

– Serves four to six –

1 shank-end, half-bone-in leg of
   lamb, 4 or 5 pounds
6 large garlic cloves
1½ teaspoons dried lavender
   flowers
1 tablespoon fresh thyme leaves

1½ tablespoons finely ground
   sea salt
2 tablespoons mixed
   peppercorns
1 tablespoon dried rosemary
1 tablespoon *herbes de Provence*

Preheat the oven to 450°F. If the butcher has not already removed the fell (parchmentlike membrane) from the lamb leg, trim it away along with all excess fat. Using the tip of a sharp knife, make 15 or so small incisions in the leg, spacing them evenly.

Place the garlic, lavender, and thyme in a small food processor and pulse until you have a thick paste. Poke a bit of the paste into each of the incisions in the lamb. Place the salt, peppercorns, dried rosemary, and *herbes de Provence* in a spice grinder and pulse until you have a coarse mix. Rub the mix all over the lamb, covering it evenly. Place the lamb on a rack in a roasting pan.

Roast the lamb for 15 minutes. Lower the heat to 350°F and continue to roast for about 1 hour, or until a thermometer inserted into the thickest part away from the bone registers 130°F for rare, 140° to 145°F for medium-rare, or 160°F for well-done. Cooking times will vary depending on the shape of the lamb and the consistent heat of your oven. Remove the lamb from the oven and let it rest for 15 minutes before carving.

Carve the lamb parallel to the bone in long, thin slices and arrange the slices on a platter. Transfer the warm sauce to a sauceboat and serve immediately.

Spicy Mint Sauce

Makes about I cup

1 (8-ounce) jar mint jelly
1 small jalapeño chile, seeded
   and minced, or to taste

¼ cup dark rum, or to taste

While the lamb is resting, combine the mint jelly, chile, and rum in a small saucepan over medium heat. Cook, stirring occasionally, for about 5 minutes, or until the jelly liquefies and the sauce is warmed through.

PLAYLIST

Music was very much a part of this experience and there was a lot of it, ranging across genres and time frames from the gutbucket blues of Bessie Smith that Sam taught me to listen to and love, to Maceo Woods's growling gospel organ, to the shining trills of Martina Arroyo and Leontyne Price. When I was back in my apartment? I was listening to Carole King, who seemed to be talking to me—"You've Got a Friend." When I was trying to hang in there no matter what, Aretha explained why I hung in—"You Make Me Feel Like a Natural Woman" (or at least how I thought a natural woman should feel). Or if I was feeling unsure, Jacques Brel and Nina Simone agreed—"Ne Me Quitte Pas." I caterwauled my way up and down my emotional roller coaster in my Jane Street apartment. At other times, my emotions changed my mental playlists. I had a mental wedding playlist (although the word had not yet been coined) that included Curtis Mayfield songs like "We've Only Just Begun" and my all-time West African favorite, "Il N'est Jamais Trop Tard," and a playlist for bad days that included every maudlin ballad known. From the dancing tunes of our raucous parties to the wailing notes of my grief, there was always music. Here are some of the songs that went (or should have gone) with the moments.

CHAPTER ONE: CLUB 81—SAMMY AND JIMMY

"Tuna de Letras"—Will Tura and Bart Peeters

"Tenth and Greenwich (Women's House of Detention)"
    —Melvin Van Peebles

"Memories Are Made of This"—Dean Martin

"Try to Remember"—Tom Jones and Jerry Orbach

"Come and Get These Memories"—Martha and the
    Vandellas

"The Way We Were"—Barbra Streisand

"Memory"—Betty Buckley

CHAPTER TWO: AND THE BABY MADE THREE

"Mockin' Hill"—Patti Page

"Tired of Being Alone"—Al Green

"Je Cherche un Homme"—Eartha Kitt

"To Be Young, Gifted and Black"—Nina Simone

"Mama Didn't Lie"—Jan Bradley

"Father and Daughter"—Paul Simon

"Fame"—Irene Cara

"Ego Tripping (There May Be a Reason Why)"—Nikki
    Giovanni

"Just Like a Woman"—Nina Simone

PLAYLIST

CHAPTER THREE: BANTAM SAM WAS THE MAN

"Home Is Where the Hatred Is"—Esther Phillips

"Your Love Is So Doggone Good"—Esther Phillips

"Peace Be Still"—James Cleveland and the Southern
California Community Choir

"Send in the Clowns"—Mabel Mercer

"Solitude"—Billie Holiday

"Amazing Grace"—Maceo Woods

"T'ain't Nobody's Bizness If I Do"—Bessie Smith

"Me and My Gin"—Bessie Smith

"I Shall Be Released"—Nina Simone

"A City Called Heaven, 'I Am a Poor Pilgrim of
Sorrow'"—Martina Arroyo

CHAPTER FOUR: OH, THE PEOPLE YOU'LL MEET!

"We've Only Just Begun"—Curtis Mayfield

"You've Got a Friend"—Carole King

"Send in the Clowns"—Mabel Mercer

"Why Did I Choose You?"—Mabel Mercer

"This Joint Is Jumpin'"—Fats Waller

"Love and Happiness"—Al Green

"Signed, Sealed, Delivered I'm Yours"
—Stevie Wonder

"Superstition"—Stevie Wonder

"Suzanne"—Nina Simone

"(You Make Me Feel Like) A Natural Woman"
   —Aretha Franklin

"At Last"—Etta James

CHAPTER FIVE: OH, THE PLACES YOU'LL GO! WEST SIDE RAMBLES

"Let's Stay Together"—Al Green

"Midnight Train to Georgia"—Gladys Knight and
   the Pips

"Dixie/Up on the Roof"—Stuff

"Lift Every Voice and Sing"—Stuff

"Sunday in Savannah"—Mabel Mercer

"Chase Me, Charlie"—Mabel Mercer

"Wait 'til You're 65"—Mabel Mercer

"Der Erlkönig"—Jessye Norman

"Vissi d'Arte"—Leontyne Price

"Dio Che Nell'alma Infondere"—Plácido Domingo

CHAPTER SIX: WANDERLUST: SONOMA, HAITI, AND PARIS

"*Choucoune*"—Moune de Rivel

"*Haiti Chéri*"—Jacques Sauveur Jean

"Haiti"—Lolita Cuevas

"*Marabout de mon coeure-bonsoir dam*"—Toto Bissainthe

"Ain't No Mountain High Enough"—Marvin Gaye,
   Tammi Terrell

"Paris au Mois d'Août"—Charles Aznavour

"I Love Paris"—Ella Fitzgerald

"J'ai Deux Amours"—Josephine Baker

"California Dreamin'"—The Mamas and the Papas

"California Love"—Tupac Shakur

CHAPTER SEVEN: TITINE AND TABASCO

"Tous les Garçons et les Filles"—François Hardy

"Ne Me Quitte Pas"—Jacques Brel or Nina Simone

"Un Homme et une Femme"—Francis Lai

"Neither One of Us"—Gladys Knight and the Pips

"Didn't We"—Barbra Streisand

"La Mer"—Yves Montand

"Les Marchés de Provence"—Gilbert Bécaud

"Je Cherche après Titine"— Yves Montand

"Non, Je ne Regrette Rien"—Edith Piaf

"Lilac Wine"—Nina Simone

CHAPTER EIGHT: SOUL-FULL

"I Will Survive"—Gloria Gaynor

"There Is a Balm in Gilead"—Martina Arroyo and
    Dorothy Maynor

"Come Ye Disconsolate"—Roberta Flack and Donny
    Hathaway

"O Death (Death in the Morning)"—Marion Williams

"Ain't No Sunshine"—Bill Withers

"I'll Fly Away"—The Blind Boys of Alabama or the
    Preservation Hall Jazz Band

PLAYLIST

"Amazing Grace"—Aretha Franklin

"Who Is He (And What Is He to You)?"—Bill Withers

"Drown in My Own Tears"—Aretha Franklin or Ray
    Charles

"For the Good Times"—Al Green

CHAPTER NINE: AFTERMATH

"Solid"—Nick Ashford and Valerie Simpson

"Go Tell It on the Mountain"—Smokey Robinson and the
    Miracles

"Scandal in the Family"—Maya Angelou

"Peas and Rice"—Maya Angelou

"Three Little Birds"—Bob Marley

"How Can You Mend a Broken Heart"—Al Green

"Blame It on My Youth"—Mabel Mercer

CHAPTER TEN: IT AIN'T OVER 'TIL IT'S OVER!

"Just My Imagination"—The Temptations

"It Is Well with My Soul"—Harding University Concert
    Choir

"Hallelujah"—Leonard Cohen

"Hallelujah Chorus"—George Frideric Handel

"Doni Doni"—Bembeya Jazz National

"How I Got Over"—Stars of Faith

"Here Comes the Sun"—Nina Simone

ACKNOWLEDGMENTS

How do you thank a lifetime's worth of friends? It is impossible and awkward. Do you just go down the list of those who offered specific assistance or thank those who kept you on the planet during the writing of the book with calls, food, and encouragement? Do you thank those from years ago who, with a word, a gesture, or a kindness, made things better on a bad day? Or do you limit yourself to those who moved you forward on the road or held your hand while you wrote? The following is a little bit of all.

Certainly the list of folks to be acknowledged has to begin with my late parents, Rhoda and Jesse Harris, without whom I would not be and would not be me.

The Queens College SEEK Program and its faculty and staff past and present, especially Frank Franklin (*Ibae*), Corrine Jennings, and Doreen June Bobb; the Queens College English Department; Kami Tobitt and Tenisha McDonald. I have worked there for more than forty-six years and to say that it is home and that those I work with

ACKNOWLEDGMENTS

and have worked with have become my extended family is rank understatement.

Continuing and renewed friendships from "then" include Louise Meriwether, who simply said "Absolutely" when I asked if I should tell the story; Helen Brodie Baldwin, Jimmy's sister-in-law, who said, "Do it!," put names to faces, and reminded me of things in St. Paul-de-Vence, in Paris, and in New York; Lydia Stuckey, Maya Angelou's personal assistant and friend for more than thirty years, who said, "You'd better," answered the phone, and generously shared memories; Martina Arroyo, who shared reminiscences as well; Nick Townsend, former Queens College colleague, who gave me Durham background and insights into Sam's early life; Richard Alleman, who remembers me when—and his new husband, Tony Neufield, who knows me now—who both encourage me always; Olivia and Willy Blumer, who also remember me as I once was, as does Linda "Zap" Cohen, who reminded, encouraged, and connected me to my new "fur family"—Hatshepsut and Hannibal.

Sustaining friendships from the "now" include Ann Glickman, Toby Glickman, and Susan Leonard—the Birch Wathen Lenox Civilization team; Don Sloan and the members of the Oxford Cultural Collective; Moriba Jackson, who tweaked the cover; Kim Severson, who suggested that I write the *New York Times* article that was the genesis of this

ACKNOWLEDGMENTS

"kids." Glenn Roberts gave quiet and real support.

In Charleston, a shout-out is due Kit Bennett and Mary
Silsby, Mitchell Crosby, Linda Mayo-Perez, and Jimmy
Williams; in Nashville, Alice Randall and Caroline Randall
Williams; in Macon, Carey Pickard and Chris Howard. In
Oak Bluffs, a whoop of thanks goes out to Rhonda Con-
ley, gardener-turned-friend and partner in crime; the late
Madelon Delany Stent and her family; Keren Tonnensen,
Charlayne Hunter-Gault, Gretchen Tucker Underwood,
Robin Bolles, Sandye Grymes, Mitzi Pratt, Flip Scipio, and
Dorria Bell; and the entire Vineyard krewe of Jessica. In
Brooklyn, the stalwarts Elaine Greenstein and Jose Medina
and Martha Mae Jones all keep the phone ringing, lure me
out to dinner, and generally keep me on the planet.

My international family: Patricia Wilson and the Breteil/
Levi/Desportes clan in Paris; Haroldo and Mary Costa; Ger-
soney Azevedo, Ekede Sinha, and all at Casa Branca, in Rio
and Bahia, Brazil, the Allus, worldwide; Dana and Christian
Sardet; and the Komaclo/Houemavo/Grimaud/Swallow
families in West Africa and England are all life sustainers.

The members of my blood family are too numerous to
note, but they are owed thanks, especially those to whom I
am most connected: Gail "Asantawaa" Harris, James Eliott
Harris, and Vanessa Abukusumo-Whitney.

My adopted New Orleans family grows larger each year,

but the matrix remains Kerry Moody; the extended Costa family, especially the newest arrival, Henry "the Falcon" Stout; Daphne Derven; Michele Jean-Pierre; Lolis Eric Elie; Amanda McFillen; Gail McDonough; and "Aunt" Leah Chase and the humongous Chase clan, who has adopted me, as has the Lucullus crew—Michelle, Rebecca, "Chippy," and Warren.

My "saints" keep my life running what passes for smoothly: Eddie Garcia, my sainted mailman, who keeps my mail coming when I don't know whether I'm coming or going; David Amaral, my sainted plumber on the Vineyard; Lionel, who can repair anything; and "Bob" Toussaint, Joe Oliver, and Leadfoot Louie, who get me around on time.

Dr. Lerner and staff keep me smiling; Dr. Donald Moore and staff keep me alive; and Dr. John Mastrobattista and Sita keep me seeing the pages. I am indebted to them all.

And then, there are Olive Allu, Don Sloan, Eluned Roberts Schweitzer, Jan Bradford, Abby Hirsch, Jocelyn Brown, Ann Glickman, Olive "Aceituna" Tomlinson, Patricia Lawrence-Haughton, Patrick Dunne, and Wendy Taucher—readers who encouraged, reminded, and gently supported.

None of this would have happened without my dream team of Susan Ginsburg, my agent and sister/friend who believes in me when I don't believe in myself, and her indefatigable assistant, Stacey Testa, who recognizes my voice whenever I call and gets me through.

ACKNOWLEDGMENTS

At Scribner, which is housed in the Simon & Schuster building where I was published for twenty-one years, I feel very Edna St. Vincent Millay, "round again 'til I've come back to where I started from." There, I owe thanks to Sally Howe, editorial assistant; Laura Wise, production editor; and copy editor Beverly H. Miller, who have kept me on target, on time, and coherent. I thank Jessica Yu, publicist, for getting the word out and helping me with the intricacies of social media.

Executive editor Kathryn Belden, my editor and my friend, holds my hand when I need it, lets me cry when I need to, and forces me to be a better writer and, more often than not, a better person than I think I am. I will be forever in her debt.

Finally, all praises are due the Lord, Orisha, and creative spirits who keep the ink flowing. I am grateful to all. To those whom I omitted, I offer my sincere apologies. I'm old enough to claim that age-related forgetfulness is the reason.

Oak Bluffs, Martha's Vineyard, September 26, 2016

ABOUT THE AUTHOR

Jessica B. Harris is one of a handful of African Americans who have achieved prominence in the culinary world. She holds a PhD from NYU, teaches English at Queens College, and lectures internationally. Her articles have appeared in *Vogue*, *Food & Wine*, *Essence*, and *The New Yorker*, among other publications. She has made numerous television and radio appearances and has been profiled in *The New York Times*. Considered one of the preeminent scholars of the food of the African Diaspora, Harris has been inducted into the James Beard Who's Who in Food and Beverage in America, received an honorary doctorate from Johnson & Wales University, holds awards from sources too numerous to note, and was recently "the intellectual architect" of the Smithsonian's National Museum of African American History and Culture to conceptualize its cafeteria.